A Guide
Enrichment of Laboratory
Rodents

Contributors and affiliations:

Christina Winnicker, DVM, MPH, DACLAM
Associate Director, Institute of Comparative Medicine
Columbia University, Zuckerman Mind Brain Behavior Institute

Brianna Gaskill, PhD
Assistant Professor, Animal Welfare
Department of Comparative Pathobiology
Purdue University

Joseph P. Garner, PhD
Associate Professor, Department of Comparative Medicine
Courtesy Associate Professor, Department of Psychiatry
and Behavioral Sciences
Stanford University

Kathleen R. Pritchett-Corning, DVM, DACLAM
Senior Clinical Veterinarian, Animal Resources
Harvard University Faculty of Arts and Sciences

Published by Charles River Laboratories, February 2016

Table of contents

Introduction

A well-designed behavioral husbandry program should accommodate the innate physiological and behavioral needs of the laboratory animals involved. One component of such a program is environmental enrichment, which refers to changes in the environment that accommodate the innate physiological and behavioral needs of animals.[1,2] The primary goal of environmental enrichment is to make the animals feel secure and give them a sense of control within a complex, challenging environment. Environmental enrichments can encourage behaviors desirable in the laboratory[3] while decreasing the incidence of abnormal behaviors.[4,5,6,7,8,9,10,cited by 11] An effective enrichment system increases the diversity of species-typical behavior, positive utilization of the environment and the ability to cope with challenges.

When designing a behavioral husbandry program, it's important to note that the psychological components of a stressor (i.e., if it can be predicted and controlled) generally have a much greater impact on an animal's mental and physical well-being than the physiology of the stressor. For instance, animals that cannot predict, control or escape from electric shocks show profound changes, such as immune suppression, while animals that can predict, control or escape from the same shocks do not show such profound physiological repercussions.[12,13,14,15]

Husbandry systems may provide for an animal's physical needs, but if they do so by providing a homogenous, uncontrollable and/or barren environment, they fail to meet an animal's psychological need for control (e.g., over temperature, food choice, escape from human predators, mate choice, etc.). Generally, the more biologically relevant a material or object is (by addressing an animal's specific behavioral needs), the more likely the material is to be truly enriching.[16]

Another important component of an effective behavioral husbandry program is behavioral management. Behavioral management is the acclimation of animals to the laboratory environment, including (but not limited to) habituation to handling and common laboratory procedures and the use of operant conditioning or other behavioral strategies to elicit cooperation with procedures, encourage desirable behaviors and discourage abnormal or otherwise undesirable behaviors in the research environment.

Handling acclimation can decrease stress and allow for recovery from research procedures more quickly.[17] Habituation to research procedures can lead not only to better welfare but to better science. For example, Fisher rat pups handled daily from birth to weaning developed higher primary and secondary serum antibody titers to flagellin antigen than did unmanipulated controls,[18] and Holzman rats held and stroked for 10 minutes daily from weaning to 45 days of age survived significantly longer following SQ injection of cancer cells.[19] While operant conditioning can be used to encourage cooperation during procedures, it is infrequently used as a technique in rodents, but may be useful under certain research paradigms.

Consequently, the fundamental goal of the behavioral husbandry program, comprised of both enrichment and behavioral management, is to return control to the animal over stressors that it perceives and is motivated to overcome. By giving the animal control, stressors have less impact on the animal's biology (and hence less impact on the science a research animal may be involved in). Behavior, particularly in mammals, is adaptive. This plasticity can be used to provide the animal with control, or even the perception of control, over their environment, which will allow them to better cope with potential stressors.

Understanding Behavior

If the goals of a behavioral husbandry program are to encourage natural behaviors, decrease abnormal behaviors, and improve health and psychological well-being, then a thorough understanding of the animals' physical, social and psychological requirements is necessary.

In general, the natural habitat and behavioral repertoire of the species that are utilized in the laboratory is known. Their natural habitats, including temperature, landscape, humidity and available resources, have shaped their behavioral drives. Similarly, their sensory modalities, circadian patterns of activity, offspring-rearing methods, typical diet and self-identified threats to well-being will all influence their behavioral repertoire. These factors may also change significantly over their lifetimes, as the activities and resources that are important to a juvenile may not be suitable for a reproductive adult or aging individual. By considering the natural and individual behaviors of the animals that they aim to enrich, researchers can develop enrichments that are biologically and behaviorally relevant.

Choosing and Evaluating Enrichments

A good strategy to follow when deciding on an enrichment strategy is to make sure the objects or materials are 1) safe for the animals; 2) biologically secure so that they will not interfere with the scientific enquiry; and 3) scientifically tested and validated, both for the research being conducted and the ethological relevance to the animal.

Making sure that an enrichment item is safe for the animals seems intuitive, but even well-intentioned enrichments can prove to be hazardous. Testing out the durability of an object, both from wear and tear inflicted by the animal and the cleaning or sterilization processes, can be done before objects are placed within the animals' environment. For example, assessing objects for sharp edges, parts that could be broken or easily dismantled by the animal, or design elements that could result in entrapment or injury can be done prior to providing the item to the animals. Simple tests like a drop test or testing the strength of seams or attachments can weed out potential problem items. Once an item is determined to be basically safe for the animals, it can be provided to a small number of pilot animals to assess its durability and utilization. (See Appendix A for a sample environmental enrichment safety assessment format.)

Scientific validation of an enrichment item should include both an evaluation of the enrichment object from the perspective of the science and the behavior of the animal. The introduction of any environmental change has the potential to introduce new scientific variables and should be carefully considered and tested before implementation. When assessing enrichments for their compatibility with research manipulations, multiple issues should be considered. For instance, can the required clinical observations be achieved? Can the animals be safely and expediently restrained for research procedures or do the environmental changes interfere? What is the enrichment item made of? Is it possible that the material will interfere with potential scientific endpoints? For example, certain wood beddings have been associated with alterations in drug-metabolizing liver enzymes,[20] and BPA, a chemical used in the creation of plastics, has been associated with multi-generational effects on reproduction.[21] Some items can be "certified," but there is no industry standard that establishes what a "certified" item is certified for, and most certification panels are toxin screens for things like aflatoxin or pesticides. For this reason, compatibility with the scientific research being undertaken still needs to be considered at the project level.

Observing Behavior

Once enrichments are developed, there is a need to assess the effectiveness of the program. If the aims of the behavioral husbandry program are to increase behavioral diversity, reduce the frequency of abnormal behavior, increase the positive utilization of the environment and increase the animals' ability to cope with challenges, then the observation and quantification of those parameters can give a measure of success.

The process of observing behavior should always begin with an ethogram — a list of behaviors and objective criteria by which they may be distinguished. Ideally ethograms are:[22]

1) *Exclusive*: An observed behavior can be characterized as one and only one entry in the ethogram, never two or more different things. This is essential for later data analysis.

2) *Exhaustive*: At any point in time, the observed behavior of the animal can be classified (even if this is as an "other" or "out of sight" category). This is particularly important for constructing time budgets and generally ensuring fair comparisons between individuals.

3) *Operationalized*: Behaviors are defined by objective criteria (e.g., one might define feeding in chickens as "the tip of the beak is within the food trough"). Although operationalized definitions may make some errors, they are objective and consistent, avoid the injection of subjectivity (especially from different observers), and allow other researchers to interpret the behavior.

Basic ethograms for most of the species discussed in this guidebook have been included to help researchers get started in this type of observation and assessment. Clearly stated, objective criteria are necessary for evaluating the effect(s) of environmental changes and for measuring changes in the psychological well-being of the animals being enriched.[23] Without such careful observations, there is no way of knowing if the enrichments provided are truly improving the welfare of animals.

The Bottom Line

Artificial environments are not controlled by the animal. Normally, behavior allows animals to control their environment. Many of these behaviors require substrate for the behavioral goal to be accomplished. An understanding of the animals' natural history and behavioral repertoire provides an idea of what substrates would be appropriate. In its most basic application, enrichment is the provision of these substrates, and the ability to elicit control over the substrate to affect the environment. The provision of ethologically relevant enrichment(s) that will be effective in the laboratory requires an understanding of the species' typical behavior, as well as making sure that the environment is safe for the animal, adhere to the biosecurity restrictions of the research environment and is compatible with the research activities and parameters.

References

1. Fernandez-Teruel, A. et al. Early-life handling stimulation and environmental enrichment — Are some of their effects mediated by similar neural mechanisms? *Pharmacology Biochemistry and Behavior*. **73**, 233-245 (2002).

2. Gaskill, B. N., Garner, J. P. & Pritchett-Corning, K. R. Energy reallocation to breeding performance through improved behavioral thermoregulation. *Journal of the American Association for Laboratory Animal Science*. **50**, 771 (2011).

3. Hurst, J. L. & West, R. S. Taming anxiety in laboratory mice. *Nat. Meth.* **7**, 825-826 (2010).

4. Shepherdson, D. J. in *Euroniche Conference Proceedings*, Edinburgh, Scotland (eds. Close, B. S., Dolins, F. & Mason, G. J.). 91-102 (Humane Education Centre, London, 1989).

5. Würbel, H., Chapman, R. & Rutland, C. Effect of feed and environmental enrichment on development of stereotypic wire-gnawing in laboratory mice. *Applied Animal Behaviour Science*. **60**, 69-81 (1998).

6. Bechard, A., Meagher, R. & Mason, G. Environmental enrichment reduces the likelihood of alopecia in adult C57BL/6J mice. *Journal of the American Association for Laboratory Animal Science*. **50**, 171-174 (2011).

7. Wiedenmayer, C. Causation of the ontogenetic development of stereotypic digging in gerbils. *Animal Behaviour*. **53**, 461-470 (1997).

8. Wiedenmayer, C. The early otogeny of bar-gnawing in laboratory gerbils. *Animal Welfare*. **6**, 273-277 (1997).

9. Wiedenmayer, C. Stereotypies resulting from a deviation in the ontogenetic development of gerbils. *Behavioural Processes*. **39**, 215-221 (1997).

10. Chamove, A. S. & Moodie, E. M. Are alarming events good for captive monkeys? *Applied Animal Behaviour Science*. **27**, 169-176 (1990).

11. Young, R. J. *Environmental enrichment for captive animals* (eds. Kirkwood, J. K., Hubrecht, R. C. & Roberts, E. A.). (Blackwell Science Ltd, Oxford, 2003).

12. Weiss, J. M. Somatic effects of predictable and unpredictable shock. *Psychosomatic Medicine*. **32**, 397-408 (1970).

13. Moberg, G. P. in *The biology of animal stress: Basic principles and implications for animal welfare* (eds. Moberg, G. P. & Mench, J. A.). 1-22 (CABI, Wallingford, UK, 2000).

14. Laudenslager, M. L. et al. Coping and immunosuppression - Inescapable but not escapable shock suppresses lymphocyte-proliferation. *Science*. **221**, 568-570 (1983).

15. Weiss, J. M. Effects of coping behavior with and without a feedback signal on stress pathology in rats. *Journal of Comparative and Physiological Psychology*. **77**, 22-30 (1971).

16. Würbel, H. & Garner, J. Refinement of rodent research through environmental enrichment and systematic randomization. *National Centre for the Replacement, Refinement and Reduction of Animals in Research*. **9** (2007).

17. Gartner, K. et al. Stress response of rats to handling and experimental procedures. *Laboratory Animals*. **14**, 267-274 (1980).

18. Solomon, G. F., Levine, S. & Kraft, J. K. Early Experience and Immunity. *Nature*. **220**, 821-822 (1968).

19. Newton, G., McCrary, C. & Bly, C. G. Effects of Early Experience on Response to Transplanted Tumor. *Journal of Nervous and Mental Disease*. **134**, 522-527 (1962).

20. Buddaraju, A. K. & Van Dyke, R. W. Effect of animal bedding on rat liver endosome acidification. *Comp Med*. **53**, 616-621 (2003).

21. Salian, S., Doshi, T. & Vanage, G. Perinatal exposure of rats to Bisphenol A affects the fertility of male offspring. *Life Sciences*. **85**, 742-752 (2009).

22. Martin, P. & Bateson, P. *Measuring behavior: an introductory guide*. (Cambridge University Press, Cambridge, 2004).

23. Galef, B. G., Sorge, R. E. Use of PVC Conduits by Rats of Various Strains and Ages Housed Singly and in Pairs. *Journal of Applied Animal Welfare Science*. **3**, 279-292 (2000).

PART 1

Abnormal Behavior

Problem Behaviors versus Abnormal Behaviors

The distinction between problem behaviors and abnormal behaviors (and maladaptive and malfunctional abnormal behaviors) is critical to understanding the impact of the behavior on the animal's well-being, potential scientific effects and correct approaches to management.[1] Problem behaviors are undesirable to the owner, care staff or end user of an animal.[1]

They may be undesirable because they are:
1) a direct well-being concern (e.g., self-injurious behaviors); 2) a safety concern for other animals or for human handlers (e.g., aggression); 3) an impediment to interaction and handling (e.g., disobedience or fear of humans); 4) unsightly or annoying (e.g., "elimination disorders" in companion animals or excessive vocalization such as screeching in parrots); or 5) destructive and costly in terms of the enclosure.

Because problem behaviors are defined solely in terms of their impact on humans, their meaning in terms of well-being has to be assessed on a case-by-case basis. However, because these behaviors impact humans, they tend to be the ones that get the most attention in a husbandry system. Furthermore, while some problem behaviors are also abnormal behaviors (e.g., self-injurious behaviors), many are not (e.g., chewing in puppies) — and many abnormal behaviors may not be considered as problems at all (e.g., sexual bonding to humans in parrots). Taking inappropriate steps to correct a problem behavior that is not a well-being concern can itself cause a welfare issue. It may be possible to redirect a problem behavior to a less inconvenient form (e.g., redirecting a puppy to chew on toys rather than books), but some problem behaviors are, from the animal's point of view, fundamentally necessary to control the world, and interfering with them (however benignly) inevitably causes welfare issues.

In contrast to the human-centered definition of a problem behavior, abnormal behaviors are defined from the animal's point of view as being quantitatively or qualitatively unusual.

This definition may be somewhat vague, but there is no one thing that makes a behavior abnormal, and attempts to define abnormal behavior in terms of a single concept (e.g., neurophysiological pathology) inevitably leave out many important behaviors or important avenues to resolving them.[1] Instead, abnormal behavior can be defined holistically, using the same "weight of evidence" approach (and the same criteria) as is used to identify abnormal behaviors in humans.[2] Thus, the more of the following criteria a behavior meets, the more likely it is to be abnormal and to be an indicator of a well-being problem:

1. *Unnatural*: Is the behavior seen only in captivity (e.g., stereotypies)?

2. *Unexpected*: If seen in the wild as well as captivity, is the behavior performed either excessively (e.g., screeching in parrots) or under inappropriate circumstances (e.g., infanticide in mice)?

3. *Non-functional*: Does the behavior lack a functional benefit to the animal in terms of survival and reproduction or does it impair the animal's survival (e.g., ulcerative dermatitis in mice), reproductive success (e.g., stereotypies in mink) or other functional behaviors (e.g., barbering in mice affects social interactions)?

4. *Infrequent*: Does the behavior occur only in a subset of individuals (e.g., barbering in rodents)?

5. *Distress*: Does the behavior induce pain or distress in the animal or its companions (e.g., unmitigated conspecific aggression)?

Maladaptive versus Malfunctional Abnormal Behavior

Having identified a behavior as abnormal, the critical distinction to be made in terms of assessing the animal's well-being and establishing strategies to alleviate the behavior is whether the behavior is "maladaptive" or "malfunctional."[1,2]

Maladaptive behaviors are the result of abnormal or uncontrollable environmental stimuli acting on a normal animal to produce unexpected (i.e., excessive or inappropriate) behavioral responses. Maladaptive behaviors are, by definition, never unnatural, but may meet all of the remaining three criteria for abnormal behavior. The well-being concerns arising from maladaptive behaviors stem from the fact that the animal is highly motivated to attain a goal that cannot be met (and is therefore likely to be frustrated and distressed),[2,3,4] in addition to secondary consequences (such as illness or injury).[1] Maladaptive behaviors can be cured (and prevented) if the underlying cues are addressed; some examples of strategies to do so are provided in the following section.

In contrast to maladaptive behaviors, malfunctional behaviors are those where pathology or the environment has induced a pathological change in the animal's neurophysiology or neuroendocrinology. Malfunctional behaviors therefore tend to be unnatural, are less likely to be unexpected and generally meet the other criteria of abnormal behavior. The main well-being concern is the underlying pathology and any secondary issues, such as injury.[1,2] In mice, good examples are ulcerative dermatitis (UD), stereotypies and barbering, with the latter two also seen in rats. Because the underlying pathology in many malfunctional behaviors can be irreversible (e.g., in knockout mice, where these behaviors may be a result of the genes that have been bred out),[5] these behaviors are important indicators of well-being issues at a population level (essentially as "behavioral scars,"[6] even though they may not be "curable" in individual animals). With malfunctional behaviors being potentially incurable in individual animals, prevention is the best strategy. In mice, only stereotypy is well understood, though our understanding of barbering and ulcerative dermatitis is advancing rapidly. In the case of stereotypy, and potentially barbering, enrichment seems to be helpful. However, barbering (and perhaps ulcerative dermatitis) appears to have much more to do with a metabolic pathogenesis,[7] and thus dietary refinements may ultimately prove the most helpful prevention strategy.

Maladaptive Behaviors

Mice and rats

In mice, good examples of maladaptive behaviors include excessive aggression and infanticide. Aggression in mice, in brief, is promoted by warmer temperatures,[8] by physical cues that allow mice to ambush each other,[9,10] by odor cues (or the lack of them)[11] and by larger group sizes.[12] Because maladaptive behaviors are driven by external cues, they are readily resolved by removing these cues or giving the animal control over them. For instance, in the case of aggression, preserving nest odor cues during cage change[11] and reducing group size (but not increasing floor area)[12] reduce aggression.

Infanticide is poorly understood in laboratory mice. The majority of studies come from wild house mice within a couple of generations of housing in the lab. In wild (or near-wild) house mice, infanticide in males and female adults is driven by very different cues (for a full review, see Weber, E. M. & Olsson, I. A. S.[13]). Male mice will kill pups that they have not fathered, thus their propensity for infanticide decreases as a function of time since ejaculation (up until the expected birth date of a litter they should have fathered) and is completely suppressed by cohabitation with a female with which they have mated — in fact, male mice in the wild play a major role in the parental care of weaned pups.[14,15,16] Wild females, on the other hand, use infanticide as a means to compete with other females in the same territory, and alloparenting and a lack of infanticide is only seen when wild sibling females colonize a territory at the same time.[17] These data might argue that monogamous breeding pairs would minimize infanticide. Several females to one male is a common breeding configuration in laboratory mice and is successful in producing more pups per cage than a cage with only one female.[18] Therefore, it is unclear to what degree these behavioral responses have been bred out of laboratory mice, especially when higher mortality is seen in some strains in harem paradigms,[18] and most likely inadvertent selection has occurred in at least some mouse strains to minimize these responses.

Food grinding, in both mice and rats, is another abnormal and problematic behavior. Mice and rats "grind" excessive amounts of food pellets into a fine dust (called orts) which piles up on the cage floor. This behavior can become an even larger problem when rodents are housed on wire bottom floors and cannot re-forage for food once the hopper has been depleted. Based on the little information that is known about food grinding, it can be categorized as a maladaptive behavior, since food wastage is seen in both captive and wild rodents.[19,20,21,22,23] The mechanisms that lead to the development of food grinding are not known, as well as whether or not some of the pellet is consumed during this behavior. Food hardness and pellets made of finely ground particles have been found to decrease the overall amount of orts collected[20,24] and pellet diameter has been found to increase it.[20]

<u>Hamsters</u>

While aggressiveness among hamsters isn't an abnormal behavior, per se, decreasing or at least mitigating it in the laboratory environment is desirable. The provision of structural enrichment, specifically a tunnel, has been shown to decrease aggressiveness.[25,26] In one study, socially housed animals were found to attempt to bite handlers less than individually housed hamsters.[26] In addition, a slow approach, allowing sleeping hamsters to awaken before handling them, then using a scoop technique (rather than scruffing), may decrease aggressiveness associated with handling.

Malfunctional Behaviors

<u>Mice and rats</u>

Stereotypies in rats and mice (e.g., bar mouthing, route tracing, jumping and back-flipping) and barbering are reviewed extensively elsewhere.[27] Both stereotypies and barbering are associated with evidence of abnormal function in different cortico-striatal circuits in the brain.[28] However, the initial causes for these changes in brain function may be quite different for the two behaviors. Stereotypies in mice appear to stem primarily from escape attempts, and so are intensified by aspects of the

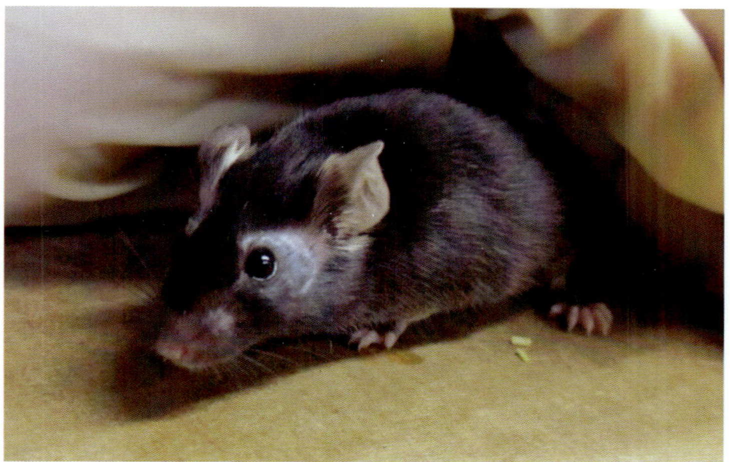

Figure 1: Mouse barbering. Charles River, 2012

cage which would increase escape motivation and reduced (to a degree) by enrichment.[29] Barbering (*Figure 1*) appears to be a more physiological illness, and has been validated as a model of human compulsive hair pulling (trichotillomania).[30] It can be reliably induced in C57Bl/6J mice with dietary interventions,[31] and prevented and cured (to a degree) by dietary supplements.[7] Barbering also appears to be related to general stressors in the environment,[30,32] and accordingly is reduced by enrichment in mice.[33] Contrary to received wisdom, barbering has been repeatedly shown to not be a "dominance behavior."[32,34]

Very recently it has been shown that UD in mice is the product of abnormal grooming that can be detected months before the onset of the disease (*Figure 2*). In these mice, it is exacerbated by the same diet as barbering and appears to be an alternative expression of the same pathogenesis.[35] As previous research has not examined potential behavioral causes for UD, the ultimate triggers and any preventative strategies are currently unclear.

<u>Hamsters</u>

Gnawing of the wire bars or lid of the cage is an observed stereotypic behavior in hamsters.[26,36] While this behavior has been associated with either boredom or escape behaviors in

Figure 2: Mouse ulcerative dermatitis. Toccafondo, 2012

other species (e.g., gerbils and mice), the exact etiology in hamsters is uncertain. Either etiology is plausible, and either way the behavior is abnormal and indicative of poor welfare. In hamsters, the provision of running wheels, at least in one study, decreased the amount of observed stereotypic bar-mouthing.[37] However, the benefit of running wheels is still unclear, as the running may be a locomotor stereotypy in itself,[38] and therefore of questionable benefit. The provision of sufficient cage space or the introduction of structural complexity may be of better benefit.

<u>Gerbils</u>

Malfunctional behaviors are the product of abnormal psychology, brain development or neurochemistry induced by features of the captive environment. A good example of this is epileptic gerbils. Gerbils have not been observed having seizures in the wild, so wild gerbils either may not exhibit seizures or seizuring animals are quickly removed from the gene pool by predation. The presence of epilepsy in domesticated gerbils may be an example of abnormal brain development due to captive breeding. Seizure-prone gerbils may reliably be induced to seizure by placing them in a novel environment, but they will habituate to an environment, suggesting that the seizures are induced by arousal.[39] A detailed ethologic examination of the various behavioral elements and motor components of a gerbil seizure may be found in Cutler and Mackintosh.[40] The seizures can generally be described as tonic-clonic, and animals returned to normal behavioral patterns two-and-a-half to eight minutes after initial seizure onset. The longest portion of the seizure is described as "returning activity prior to normal behavior" and consisted of a gradual return to normal postures interspersed with "catatonic pauses" and normal and abnormal body and limb movements.[40]

In gerbils, there is one other very commonly seen malfunctional behavior — stereotypic digging — and another much less commonly seen behavior — bar chewing.[41] Digging in gerbils is associated with a number of behaviors such as grooming, foraging and exploration, but its primary purpose is construction and maintenance of the burrow system.[42,43]

Stereotypic digging develops in gerbils as early as day 24[44] and develops from bouts of normal digging, which begin when the eyes open at around day 18. The goal of this digging is the excavation of a burrow leading to a nesting chamber, which allows for retreat. In the wild, gerbils spend a great deal of time underground, allowing for safety from predators and amelioration of climactic extremes. If the animals are allowed substrate and space to dig naturalistic burrows, or given a tunnel that mimicked a burrow, such as a tunnel with a bend to allow for no light to enter a small chamber at the end, stereotypic digging is decreased or eliminated.[44] In one experiment, gerbils were observed to spend approximately 92 percent of their time in the burrow.[44] The necessary component of the burrow is the tube, or moving from an open area to a confined one, as providing animals with darkness and confinement without a tube did not decrease stereotypical digging.[44,45] Digging behavior is not related to substrate provided, as animals did not show less stereotypic digging when provided with sand in their cages as compared to wood chip bedding.[44,46]

References

1. Mills, D. S. Medical paradigms for the study of problem behaviour: a critical review. *Applied Animal Behaviour Science.* **81**, 265-277 (2003).

2. Garner, J. P. Stereotypies and other abnormal repetitive behaviors: Potential impact on validity, reliability, and replicability of scientific outcomes. *Ilar Journal.* **46**, 106-117 (2005).

3. Dawkins, M. S. From an animal's point of view — Motivation, Fitness, and Animal-Welfare. *Behavioral and Brain Sciences.* **13**, 1-61 (1990).

4. Dawkins, M. S. *Animal suffering: The science of animal welfare* (Chapman and Hall, London, UK, 1980).

5. Greer, J. M. & Capecchi, M. R. Hoxb8 is required for normal grooming behavior in mice. *Neuron.* **33**, 23-34 (2002).

6. Mason, G. J. Stereotypies and suffering. *Behavioural Processes.* **25**, 103-115 (1991).

7. Vieira, G., Lossie, A. C. & Garner, J. P. Trichotillomania and Related Body Focused Repetitive Behaviors. (Paper presented at the *Trichotillomania Learning Center 19th Annual National Conference*, Chicago, IL USA, 2012).

8. Greenberg, G. The effects of ambient temperature and population density on aggression in two inbred strains of mice, *Mus musculus. Behaviour.* **42**, 119-130 (1972).

9. Barnard, C. J., Behnke, J. M. & Sewell, J. Environmental enrichment, immunocompetence, and resistance to Babesia microti in male mice. *Physiology & Behavior.* **60**, 1223-1231 (1996).

10. Howerton, C., Garner, J. & Mench, J. Effects of a running wheel-igloo enrichment on aggression, hierarchy linearity, and stereotypy in group-housed male CD-1 (ICR) mice. *Applied Animal Behavior Science.* **115**, 90-103 (2008).

11. Van Loo, P. L. P. et al. Modulation of aggression in male mice: influence of cage cleaning regime and scent marks. *Animal Welfare*. **9**, 281-295 (2000).

12. Van Loo, P. L. P. & Mol, J. A. Modulation of aggression in male mice: influence of group size and cage size. *Physiology and Behavior*. **72**, 675-683 (2001).

13. Weber, E. M. & Olsson, I. A. S. Maternal behaviour in *Mus musculus* sp.: An ethological review. *Applied Animal Behaviour Science*. **114**, 1-22 (2008).

14. Gray, J. A. *The psychology of fear and stress* (Cambridge University Press, Cambridge, 1991).

15. Perrigo, G., Belvin, L. & Saal, F. S. V. Time and sex in the male mouse — Temporal regulation of infanticide and parental behavior. *Chronobiology International*. **9**, 421-433 (1992).

16. Perrigo, G., Belvin, L. & Saal, F. S. V. Social inhibition of infanticide in male house mice. *Ethology Ecology & Evolution*. **5**, 181-185 (1993).

17. Palanza, P., Della Seta, D., Ferrari, P. F. & Parmigiani, S. Female competition in wild house mice depends upon timing of female/male settlement and kinship between females. *Animal Behaviour*. **69**, 1259-1271 (2005).

18. Eskola, S. & Kaliste-Korhonen, E. Nesting material and number of females per cage: effects on mouse productivity in BALB/c, C57BL/6J, DBA/2 and NIH/S mice. *Laboratory Animals*. **33**, 122-128 (1999).

19. Tagliaferro, A. R. & Levitsky, D. A. Spillage behavior and thiamin deficiency in the rat. *Physiology & Behavior*. **28**, 933-937 (1982).

20. Ford, D. J. Influence of diet pellet hardness and particle size on food utilization by mice, rats and hamsters. *Laboratory Animals*. **11**, 241-246 (1977).

21. Owl, M. Y. & Batzli, G. O. The integrated processing response of voles to fibre content of natural diets. *Functional Ecology*. **12**, 4-13 (1998).

22. Kerley, G. I. H. & Erasmus, T. What do mice select for in seeds. *Oecologia*. **86**, 261-267 (1991).

23. Felicetti, L. A., Shipley, L. A., Witmer, G. W. & Robbins, C. T. Digestibility, nitrogen excretion, and mean retention time by North American porcupines (Erethizon dorsatum) consuming natural forages. *Physiological and Biochemical Zoology*. **73**, 772-780 (2000).

24. Cameron, K. M. & Speakman, J. R. The extent and function of 'food grinding' in the laboratory mouse (*Mus musculus*). *Laboratory Animals*. **44**, 298-304 (2010).

25. McClure, D. E. & Thomson, J. I. Cage enrichment for hamsters housed in suspended wire cages. *Contemporary Topics in Laboratory Animal Science*. **31**, 33 (1992).

26. Arnold, C. E. & Estep, D. Q. Laboratory Caging Preferences in Golden-Hamsters (Mesocricetus-Auratus). *Laboratory Animals*. **28**, 232-238 (1994).

27. Mason, G. in *Stereotypic Animal Behaviour: Fundamentals and Applications to Welfare* (eds. Rushen, J. & Mason, G.). (CABI, Wallingford, England, UK, 2006).

28. Garner, J. P. et al. Reverse-translational biomarker validation of Abnormal Repetitive Behaviors in mice: An illustration of the 4P's modeling approach. *Behavioural Brain Research*. **219**, 189-196 (2011).

29. Würbel, H. in *Stereotypic Animal Behaviour: Fundamentals and Applications to Welfare* (eds. Rushen, J. & Mason, G.). 86-120 (CABI, Wallingford, England, UK, 2006).

30. Garner, J. P., Weisker, S. M., Dufour, B. & Mench, J. A. Barbering (Fur and whisker trimming) by laboratory mice as a model of human trichotillomania and obsessive-compulsive spectrum disorders. *Comparative Medicine*. 54, 216-224 (2004)

31. Dufour, B. D. et al. Nutritional up-regulation of serotonin paradoxically induces compulsive behavior. *Nutritional Neuroscience.* **13**, 256-264 (2010).

32. Garner, J. et al. Social and husbandry factors affecting the prevalence and severity of barbering ('whisker trimming') by laboratory mice. *AABS.* **89**, 263-282 (2004).

33. Bechard, A., Meagher, R. & Mason, G. Environmental enrichment reduces the likelihood of alopecia in adult C57BL/6J mice. *Journal of the American Association for Laboratory Animal Science.* **50**, 171-174 (2011).

34. van de Weerd, H. A., van den Broek, F. A. R. & Beynen, A. C. Removal of vibrissae in male mice does not influence social dominance. *Behavioural Processes.* **27**, 205-208 (1992).

35. Dufour, B. D. et al. Nutritional up-regulation of serotonin paradoxically induces compulsive behavior. *Nutritional Neuroscience.* **13**, 256-264 (2010).

36. Hauzenberger, A. R., Gebhardt-Henrich, S. G. & Steiger, A. The influence of bedding depth on behaviour in golden hamsters (Mesocricetus auratus). *Applied Animal Behaviour Science.* **100**, 280-294 (2006).

37. Gebhardt-Henrich, S. G., Vonlanthen, E. M. & Steiger, A. How does the running wheel affect the behaviour and reproduction of golden hamsters kept as pets? *Applied Animal Behaviour Science.* **95**, 199-203 (2005).

38. Sherwin, C. M. Voluntary wheel running: a review and novel interpretation. *Animal Behaviour.* **56**, 11-27 (1998).

39. Laming, P. R., Elwood, R. W. & Best, P. M. Epileptic tendencies in relation to behavioral responses to a novel environment in the Mongolian gerbil. *Behav Neural Biol.* **51**, 92-101 (1989).

40. Cutler, M. G. & Mackintosh, J. H. Epilepsy and behaviour of the Mongolian gerbil: an ethological study. *Physiol Behav*. **46**, 561-566 (1989).

41. Moons, C. P. H. et al. The effect of different working definitions on behavioral research involving stereotypies in Mongolian gerbils (Meriones unguiculatus). *Journal of the American Association for Laboratory Animal Science*. **51**, 170-176 (2012).

42. Ågren, G., Zhou, Q. & Zhong, W. Ecology and social behaviour of Mongolian gerbils, Meriones unguiculatus, at Xilinhot, Inner Mongolia, China. *Animal Behavior*. **37**, 11-27 (1989).

43. Wiedenmayer, C. & Brunner, C. in *Proceedings of the International Congress on Applied Ethology* (eds. Nichelmann, M., Wierenga, H. K. & Braun, S.). 276-278 (KTBL, Darmstadt, Berlin, 1993).

44. Wiedenmayer, C. Causation of the ontogenetic development of stereotypic digging in gerbils. *Animal Behaviour.* **53**, 461-470 (1997).

45. Waiblinger, E. in *Comfortable Quarters for Laboratory Animals* (eds. Reinhardt, V. & Reinhardt, A.). 18-25 (Animal Welfare Institute, Washington, D.C., 2002).

46. Pettijohn, T. F. & Barkes, B. M. Surface choice and behavior in adult Mongolian gerbils. *Psychol Rec.* **28**, 299-303 (1978).

Natural History & Behavior

The natural history and behavioral ecology of the house mouse has been comprehensively reviewed by several authors, especially in the incredibly detailed work of Latham & Mason.[1] Here we emphasize a few key points that are essential for understanding how the laboratory mouse perceives and interacts with its lab environment.

Early mouse ancestors likely evolved in the steppes of the Caucasus Mountains of Turkey.[2] However, these animals are highly adaptable and have followed humans around the world, colonizing nearly every continent and environment.[1,3] In the wild, seeds, grains and insects make up the diet of this omnivorous prey species.[4] Vulnerability to predation has shaped the behavior and life history strategies of mice.[3] They are nocturnal, showing peaks of activity at dawn and dusk,[5,6,7] avoid brightly lit and open spaces and are cautious exploring new environments.[3,8]

Mice live in complex and variable social systems. Generally they live in loose kin groups called "demes" (*Figure 1*), which include a male, one to two breeding females (which are usually related), subadults and pups.[1,9] One male owns a territory ,but other

Figure 1: Mouse in natural habitat. Liz Bomford, Oxford Scientific

adults, including females, will defend it viciously.[9] Territories will vary in size from 80,000 square meters in the wheatfields of Australia[12] to 1-6 square meters when mice infest a house.[7,13] Territory size is based on many factors, such as seasonal temperatures[9,10] or distribution of resources.[11] The structure of the territory's environment is utilized to ambush intruders through holes, choke-points, and elevated platforms[9,14] (*Figure 2*). Subordinate, non-territory holding males will often form bachelor groups if there is difficulty dispersing.[9] Mice rely on the nest site for protection and warmth.[1,9,15] and are motivated to burrow when suitable substrate is available; these behaviors have been conserved in the common laboratory mouse.[1,16]

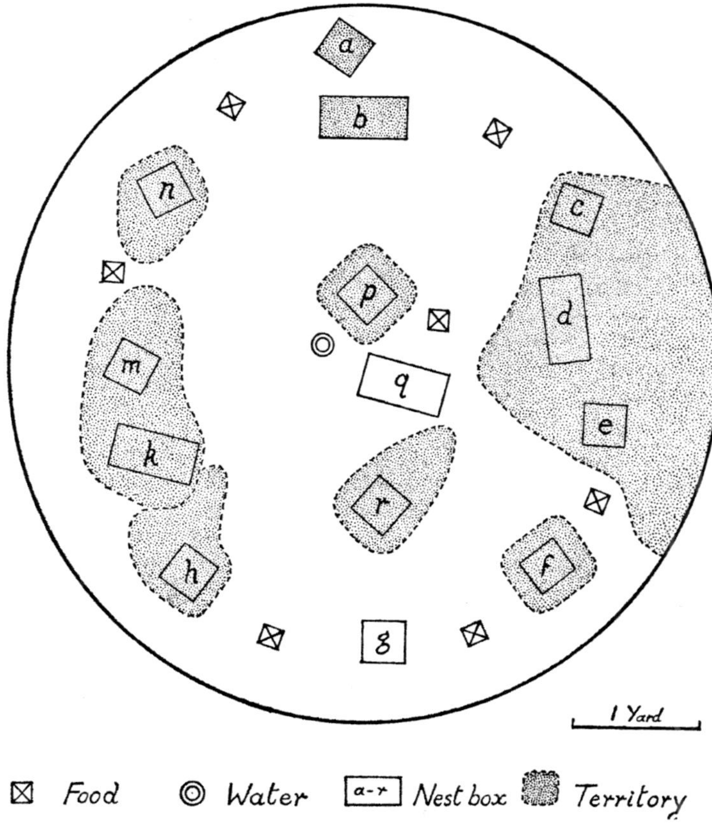

Figure 2: Mouse territory. Crowcroft P., 1973, p. 50

Mice rely on odor, sound and touch to experience the world around them.[3,17] Mice detect sound over a broader spectrum of frequencies than humans and hear well into the ultrasonic ranges.[3,17] Audible vocalizations are predominantly heard during agonistic interactions, while ultrasonic vocalizations are used more often by pups in distress and during male mating songs.[17,18] Odors are used to identify individuals and their sexual, social, and health status, as well as the location of food and predators.[19]

Mice feel the world around them by using their whiskers, which can easily discriminate textures, edges, or obstacles.[20,21,22] Touch-sensitive hairs can also be found on the body, which sense overhead cover and proximity to objects or walls. Moving through the environment while maintaining tactile contact with cover is called thigmotaxis and is especially seen when mice are in a new environment or when the animal perceives a threat (*Figure 3*).

Vision in mice is dominated by low-light movement-detection.[23] Sensitivity in low light is at the expense of acuity, with mice typically having two percent of the visual acuity of humans, though this may be far worse in some strains.[3,24] Mice cannot detect red wavelengths but are able to see in the ultraviolet end of the spectrum.[1]

Play can potentially be used as an indicator of positive welfare in confined environments.[25,26] Play is most commonly documented in juvenile rats,[27,28] and is characterized by very specific ultrasonic vocalizations. It has been suggested that the house mouse engages in social locomotor play, commonly referred to as "popcorn" behavior.[29] This behavior is seen primarily around weaning and is characterized by contagious jumping and running behaviors. This is a much more basic form of play than the rough and tumble play seen in rats, but does involve approaches and withdraws similar to what is seen in adult fighting.[29] Because these behaviors are so similar to adult fighting, the interpretation that they are play fighting and not exhibiting juvenile aggressive behavior is difficult to determine. This illustrates the enormous difficulty in appropriately identifying play.

Behavior in the Laboratory

Mouse behavior in the lab, with the exception of the widespread presence of abnormal behavior (which, if it occurs in the wild, appears to be so strongly selected against that it is rarely if ever seen), does not differ qualitatively from behavior in the wild. Instead, behavior in the lab differs from the wild quantitatively, as mice interpret and respond to cues in the lab environment as if they were in the wild. This may mean that some behaviors appear to be absent until the correct cues are presented — for instance, the full repertoire of nesting behavior can be elicited in the lab when suitable nesting material is provided[30] (*Figure 4*). This is why species-specific behavior is often considered when assessing enrichment — if the enrichment is working, it should allow the expression of new behaviors from the instinctive, wild repertoire.

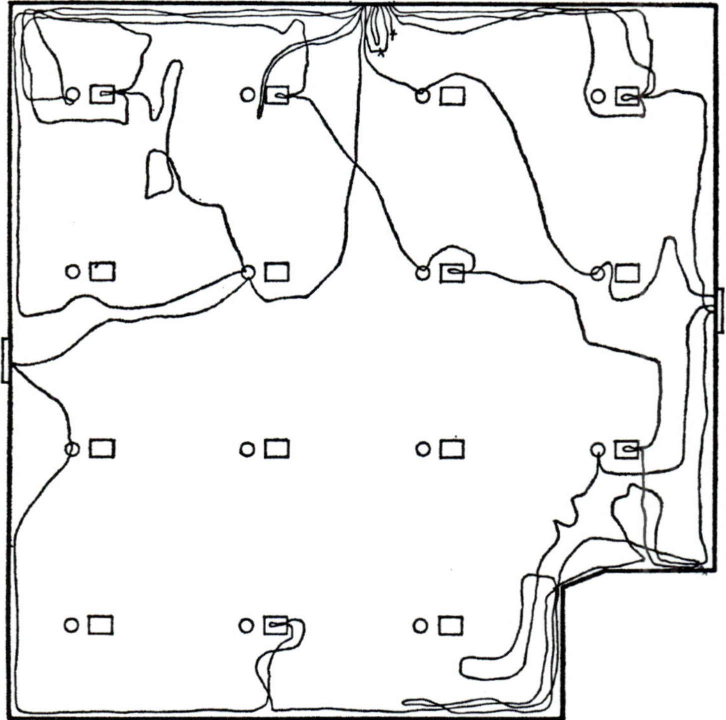

Figure 3: The movement of a female mouse during an hour of activity. Crowcroft, P., 1973, p. 42.

Figure 4: Mouse in nest. Gaskill, B. N. 2009.

Conversely, the constant presence of cues that in the wild might be fleeting or controlled by appropriate behavior can lead to the increased performance of behaviors to the point where they become management issues or even abnormal behaviors.[31] This again is an issue for enrichment because poorly-designed enrichment may introduce cues that cause behavioral problems, as is the case for shelters and mice.[32]

Similarly, good management by manipulating these cues can induce beneficial behaviors and reduce problem behaviors. Aggression provides two excellent examples. First, moving a small portion of the nest site during cage changes appears to preserve the scent marks required for positive social behavior, preventing aggression.[33] Second, mice housed in the densities and group sizes typical for the lab would normally fight until one animal owned the territory,[1,9] but this behavior is suppressed during the cold months of winter and territory holders allow other mice to share their nests.[9,10] It has been shown that typical room temperatures of 20 or 22 °C are stressfully cold for mice,[15,34,35] increasing temperature to even 25 °C induces severe aggression.[10] As a result, enrichment with nesting material provides an ideal solution — the cage temperature is maintained cool enough to prevent aggression, but the nesting material allows the mice to enjoy a warm microclimate,[36] which in turn benefits their productivity and welfare.[37]

Observing and Quantifying Behavior

Basic Ethogram

There are several published ethograms covering various mouse behaviors.[38,39,40,41] However, these ethograms do not cover all major behavioral categories and often name similarly described behaviors differently. The four ethograms cited have been combined and incorporated with other behavioral categories to produce a comprehensive ethogram at *www.mousebehavior.org.*

The fully detailed mouse ethogram (the "species ethogram") contains nearly 100 behaviors — obviously one cannot record all of them. Furthermore, the more behaviors recorded, the more observations are needed to achieve sufficient power for each behavior. Thus, the real skill in observing behavior is to choose ONLY the behaviors that one needs to answer a question, such as aggression, nesting or abnormal behavior. This collapsed list is the "experimental ethogram." An experimental ethogram adapted from a study measuring the general budget of mice in a choice test[34] can be found in *Table 1*.

Observation SOPs

Just as different research questions require different ethograms, different observation methods are better suited to different behaviors. This is a complex issue, and a key part of the training of an ethologist. An initial guide can be found in "Measuring Behavior: An Introductory Guide" by Martin and Bateson.[42] The web ethogram (*www.mousebehavior.org*) also provides some off-the-shelf SOPs for common research questions. For example, in experiments with nesting behavior, changes in abnormal behavior weren't expected, but understanding how different materials induced different behaviors and when the mice were most likely to nest meant that two different observations schemes of the same video were needed.

Table 1. Example of an Experimental Mouse Ethogram

Category	Behavior
Active	General locomotion
	Rearing
	Sniffing
Maintenance	Settling and nest-building
	Grooming
	Feeding or drinking
Inactive	Sleeping
	Still and alert

Adapted from Gaskill, B. N. et al., 2009.[34]

Description

All locomotive behavior performed on the cage lid, climbing up the cage bars by the food hopper to reach the lid, and locomotion on the floor of the cage

Seen on the floor of the cage with all of an animal's weight on its hind legs and its front legs off the ground; sniffing movements while on its hind legs commonly accompanied this behavior

Sniffing was also performed against the cage floor (ground), or in between the bars of the cage lid; Slight upward jerks of the head were seen

Turning was characterized by the animal circling on the spot within the nest, commonly preceding sleep. Gathering was characterized by the animal reaching out of the nest and pulling sawdust to the edge of the nest. Gathering was distinct from locomotion in that the hind legs did not leave the nest, and each time the animal reached out of the nest it pulled its forelegs back in.

All grooming behavior including licking the fur, grooming with the forepaws, and scratching with any limb. Grooming was usually performed in a sitting position with the animal's hind quarters in contact with the floor.

The animal would rear up to gnaw at food pellets through the bars of the hopper. The forepaws would usually be used to hold the food pellet steady. The animal would rear up and lick the nipple drinker.

The animal was motionless, and either lying curled up on its side, or sitting curled up, with its face tucked into its body and out of sight of the camera; occasionally interrupted by brief single twitches of the body.

The animal was sitting or curled up, but in contrast to sleep, the face was lifted. The animal either sat motionless, or would appear to be orientating its head to sounds outside of the cage.

Behavioral Management

Enrichment

<u>Categories of enrichment:</u>[43, 44]

As previously discussed, effective behavioral management has two sides: understanding the stressors impinging on the animal, and providing a suitable enrichment. Accordingly, one size does not necessarily fit all when it comes to environmental enrichment. Possible ideas for the enrichment of mice are detailed in this chapter, but implementation will depend on space or resource availability at each individual facility, as well as consideration of the research being conducted.

Social: Group housing for social animals, such as mice, is often an effective and relatively simple choice because of the complex and varied mental stimulation it provides,[43,45] the importance of social support to coping with stressors[46,47,48] and the inherent behavioral need many species have for social contact (*Figure 5*). In the case of highly social species, socialization at particular critical periods is usually essential for proper development,[43] and thus socially deprived animals are inherently abnormal. However, too-large or overcrowded groups can have an opposite effect, increasing aggressive interactions within the cage.[49] Similarly, subtle effects in housing design, or even other enrichments, may provide cues which

Figure 5: Group housed mice. Charles River, 2012

promote aggression, as they may be construed as resources worth fighting over. Thus, social enrichment must always be implemented carefully and with a solid understanding of the species' social behavior.

Occupational: These kinds of enrichments encourage behaviors the animal would normally spend a large portion of its time in the wild completing, such as foraging, searching for materials and building a nest. This category may include objects which challenge animals psychologically as well as physically, such as puzzle feeders. Since the purpose of this category is to engage animals and promote species-typical behaviors, this is likely to be a category which best improves the welfare of the animals and provides them with control over their environment.

• Nesting materials: Generally, nesting material is found to be beneficial to both mice and the facility using it.[50] Mice have also been shown to prefer this material over other enrichments,[51] as well as being willing to work to receive the material, indicating their motivation.[15,52] A wide range of strain differences in nest building have been documented,[15,53,54] but growing evidence suggests that this may reflect complex gene-by-environment interactions, rather than any inherent "deficit" in a particular strain. Genetic influences have been demonstrated by divergent selection of large and small nest building mice, indicating that this is highly influential.[55,56,57] However, the type of material and the amount of work needed to process it before building can also affect the resulting nest.

  i. Crinkled paper has been systematically tested[15,30,34,35,37,58] and appears to be a material many types of mice find suitable for use in building a high quality nest.[15,30] This material has been shown to alter thermoregulatory mechanisms[36] and improve breeding and food efficiency in both nude and the most commonly used mice.[15,37,59] It also does not appear to increase the incidence of eye lesions often seen in nude animals.[37,60]

  ii. Wood wool has been shown to be a preferred building material in a small subset of mice.[61] One case of increased aggression with this material has been reported with NIH/S mice. However, the mice in this study did not spend much

Figure 6: Cotton squares of varying sizes and compression.
Charles River, 2012

time in contact with the material and the authors did not describe how the material was used for nest building.[62]

iii. Compressed cotton squares can be provided in different compression strengths. Those that are less compressed are easier for poor nest building strains (e.g., C57BL/6, DBA, C3H)[15,30,63,64] to build with and result in improved breeding and food efficiency[37] (*Figure 6*). However, the short particle size of this material can cause eye lesions in nudes,[65] as well as become entangled around the feet of pups.[66]

iv. Tissue can be used by mice to build decent nests,[30] but the high dust content can be problematic for nude mice. New low-dust tissue has been introduced to the enrichment market, but few experiments have evaluated it. One study showed that mice still built better nests with other materials.[60]

• Foraging: In the wild, mice may travel a great distance to attain access to food.[67,68] In the laboratory, where food is abundant, home range size is likely to be much smaller.[9] Surprisingly, little to no work has been done looking at the benefits of foraging in mice, whether this is done by scattering food or treats or making mice gather materials for nest building. Forage boxes containing a type of nesting material[63] and/or treats that require the mice to work to attain these resources

Figure 7: Nesting foraging box. Charles River, 2012

may provide a practical and easily implemented enrichment (*Figure 7*). However, the method of delivery and the potential of increasing aggressive interactions should be considered.

• Running wheels: Wheels attached to shelters have been found to increase aggression,[32,69] and conflicting results have been found on the impact of running wheels on stereotypy development.[32,70] Most running wheels do not conveniently fit into conventional laboratory caging, making providing the option of physical exercise difficult in the laboratory. If sufficient space is available, mice prefer a large diameter wheel over a smaller one and also prefer mesh-covered wheels over rod or solid surface.[71]

• Burrowing substrate: Laboratory mice, despite not being given the opportunity to burrow for many generations, retain the motivation to express this behavior.[16] Different materials to dig in have not been evaluated, but dampened peat was used by Sherwin et al.[16] Providing peat in common laboratory housing is impractical, but mice may benefit behaviorally and thermally from burrowing in deep bedding or substrates.[72] Anecdotally, mice housed in deep aspen bedding do burrow under the surface of the bedding.

 **For a video on mice burrowing in bedding,
visit www.criver.com/behavior**

Figure 8: Gnawing devices – natural and synthetic. Charles River, 2012

• Gnawing materials: Rodents are characterized by their continuously growing front teeth and must gnaw constantly to wear them down. This is likely to be a good area to provide mice with an enrichment that meets a species-specific behavioral need.

i. Natural: Only one study has investigated the correlation between gnawing behavior (by increasing food hardness) and the development of wire-gnawing stereotypies.[73] No alteration to stereotypy development was observed based on this treatment. Other types of natural gnawing substrates, such as wood chew sticks or wood chips (*Figure 8*), are common for pet mice and other rodents, but actual utilization of these products, as well as any benefits associated with their use, have not been properly tested in the lab environment. However, potential concerns of natural estrogens present in different wood types may limit the use of these items in some experiments.

ii. Synthetic: Other commercial products that avoid the potential estrogenic confounds of natural products are available. Nylon chew bones are one commonly used option. Anecdotally, mice do not tend to utilize nylon gnawing materials to the extent that rats do, which may be why the utilization and potential benefit of these products has yet to be quantified in the literature.

Physical environment: Environmental enrichments in this category are structures the animals are housed in and with. This can include the type and size of cage they are kept in to physical structures placed inside. This is a popular category of enrichment provision because it makes the enclosure "look" enriched, but oftentimes the objects employed do not necessarily promote many of the goals of enrichment and may, in fact, increase unwanted behaviors.

- Enclosure:

i. Size: Home range size in wild house mice relies on many factors, but food availability is likely one of the most influential factors.[74] The mouse cage space literature often confounds cage space with group size, making it difficult to tease apart these factors. One study by Van Loo et al.[75] investigated these variables and found that group size may be more influential on overall aggression than space allocation per mouse. Improvements in physiological or immunological well-being seen with increased stocking density may be simply due to reduced thermal stress from huddling. Considering that mice are thigmotactic and find brightly lit and open areas aversive,[3,8] it is unlikely that large amounts of cage space will be highly enriching or practically applied in this species.

Figure 9: Socially housed mice with plastic shelter. Charles River, 2012

ii. Complexity: Improving cage complexity or overall quality has been found to improve responses to distress, learning and memory, brain physiology, and reduce tumor growth.[49,76,77,78,79] However, introducing complexity always runs the risk of creating choke points and other ambush sites that can induce aggression, which in turn can have secondary consequences on many aspects of stress physiology.[14,32] Nevertheless, with due care to avoid aggression, this approach would be more beneficial than simply increasing the quantity of space alone.

• Accessories:

i. Shelters: The little research that has looked at shelter enrichment has investigated the impact of plastic shelters (*Figure 9*) on increased aggression.[32,69] These authors suggest that this is due to hard shelters being a highly valued resource that introduces ambush points. Besides increased aggression, plastic shelters (without wheels) may provide some positive effects, such as increased longevity.[69] Other shelters, such as paper huts, or differences between flat-top and round-top shelters, have not been investigated. Although this type of enrichment may be problematic in highly aggressive strains and males, shelters may be beneficial for females or singly housed mice.

ii. Tunnels or tubes: Provision of paper tubes has been found to reduce wire-gnawing stereotypies in mice.[73] This may be because they offer cover that addresses a mouse's thigmotactic drive, and thus provide some psychological improvement in welfare. Providing tubes within the cage may also be beneficial because the mice are familiar with the structure when utilized for handling purposes.[80]

iii. Climbing structure: Climbing structures such as ladders, ramps, ropes or hammocks are more commonly used for pet rodent enclosures. Indeed, the behavioral need to climb is evident to anyone who has observed much mouse behavior in the laboratory cage. However, there is little research on this enrichment that distinguishes climbing from general structural complexity. Furthermore, the motivation for climbing on the cage lid is, at least in part, driven by escape attempts.[81]

iv. Shelves: Shelves have been used to increase usable cage floor space as well as increase vertical complexity. This enrichment has also been designed to provide mice with the ability to avoid cage flooding. Other benefits have not yet been studied.[82] It should be noted, however, that shelves can also provide mice with the ability to ambush each other, inducing aggression and disruption of social hierarchies.[14]

v. Balls or marbles: These types of objects are likely not enriching to mice, and the burying behavior observed is considered to be anxiety- or fear-driven.[83] Thus, there are better enrichments that can be provided that do not elicit negatively associated behaviors.

vi. Rattles: The use and impact of shower curtain hooks as rattles has not been tested. However, the fact that this enrichment does not directly address a species-specific behavioral need means that it is unlikely that rattles will be very beneficial.

Sensory: Mice have different primary senses than humans; therefore, enrichments that address any of these senses should be methodically considered and may be difficult to implement.

• Olfactory: Scent being one of the primary senses in mice again presents a possibility of providing a biologically relevant enrichment. Mice can easily become skilled at complex learning tasks that involve discriminating between different smells.[22] However, there is the possibility of eliciting negative behaviors depending on the scent provided. Predator-related smells are likely to induce fear and anxiety,[84,85] and providing unknown mouse odors into the home cage increases territoriality and potentially aggressive interactions.[86,87] Scent may be most useful indirectly, such as in cage cleaning; it has been shown that moving bedding from the nest site (but not latrine sites) in the cage reduces aggression following cage changes.[33]

• Tactile: A mouse's vibrissae are extremely sensitive and can distinguish different grades of sand paper[21] and many other textures.[22] However, the implementation of different textures as environmental enrichment has not been investigated.

Nutritional: Implementation of nutritional enrichments in laboratory species may be difficult, depending on the research the animals are being used for. Obviously, providing food enrichments may confound or complicate nutritional studies or studies in which food consumption is being measured.

• Delivery: The method of delivery for any type of enrichment is a detail that should always be considered. Dominant individuals are likely to monopolize access to resources, especially when highly valued. Therefore, scattering nutritional items may be the best way of avoiding aggression and providing subordinate animals with access to enrichment while also encouraging foraging behavior.

• Type:

  i. Natural: Seeds, mealworms and grain are all nutritional enrichments that are typical of what a mouse would consume in the wild.[4,88] These items have been found to be highly favored by mice.

  ii. Processed: Many commercial products exist, including compressed flavored pellets, gel treats or crumbles (which are generally sugar based), and are useful for positive reinforcement training. The usefulness of these items as foraging substrate has not been systematically assessed.

Novelty: The use of novel enrichments, or rotating enrichments, is more commonly used in the zoo setting than with mice in the laboratory. Mice are neophobic, meaning that they are initially cautious to investigate a novel object, and so the initial presentation of even a beneficial object may induce a brief period of conflict or anxiety. Therefore, constantly rotating novel enrichments is likely not a good way of enriching mice.

Recommended Behavioral Husbandry Program

Hopefully this chapter has conveyed the rich complexity of mouse behavior in the laboratory. If so, it should be clear that there is not a magic solution for all mice in all facilities. Instead, the general principles presented here should help tailor husbandry programs to the particular issues in a given facility. Remember that in creating a well-designed enrichment program, it is essential to assess the behavioral needs of the animals and the potential cues leading to problem or abnormal behaviors, and to ensure that any strategies implemented to modify or alleviate said behaviors will be biologically relevant.

Based on the information previously presented on mouse behavior and researched enrichments, It can be concluded that there are few circumstances where crinkled paper nesting material would not be the first choice for mouse enrichment. Therefore, crinkled nesting material is most likely the best single item that can be given to laboratory mice, based on the widespread benefits without any yet observed complications.

References

1. Latham, N. & Mason, G. From house mouse to mouse house: The behavioural biology of free-living Mus musculus and its implications in the laboratory. *Applied Animal Behaviour Science*. **86**, 261-289 (2004).

2. Schwarz, E. & Schwarz, H. K. The Wild and Commensal Stocks of the House Mouse, *Mus musculus Linnaeus. Journal of Mammalogy*. **24**, 59-72 (1943).

3. Jennings, M. et al. Refining rodent husbandry: The mouse — Report of the Rodent Refinement Working Party. *Laboratory Animals*. **32**, 233-259 (1998).

4. Ward, R. J. in *Biology of the house mouse* (ed. Berry, R. J.). 255-266 (Academic Press Inc, London, 1981).

5. Gordon, C. J., Becker, P. & Ali, J. S. Behavioral thermoregulatory responses of single- and group-housed mice. *Physiology & Behavior.* **65**, 255-262 (1998).

6. Rowe, F. in *Biology of the house mouse* (ed. Berry, R. J.). 575-590 (Academic Press, London, 1981).

7. *Southern, H. N. House mice*. (Oxford University Press, London, 1954).

8. Gray, J. A. *The psychology of fear and stress*. (Cambridge University Press, Cambridge, 1991).

9. Crowcroft, P. *Mice all over.* (G.T. Foulis and CO LTD, London, 1966).

10. Greenberg, G. The effects of ambient temperature and population density on aggression in two inbred strains of mice, *Mus musculus. Behaviour.* **42**, 119-130 (1972).

11. Gray, S. J., Jensen, S. P. & Hurst, J. L. Effects of resource distribution on activity and territory defence in house mice, *Mus domesticus. Animal Behaviour.* **63**, 531-539 (2002).

12. Chambers, I., Singleton, G. & Krebs, C. Movements and social organisation of wild house mice (*Mus domesticus*) in the wheatlands of northwestern Australia. *Journal of Mammology.* **81**, 59-69 (2000).

13. Young, H., Strecker, R. & Emlen, J. Localisation of activity in two indoor populations of house mice, *Mus musculus. Journal of Mammology.* **31**, 403-410 (1950).

14. Barnard, C. J., Behnke, J. M. & Sewell, J. Environmental enrichment, immunocompetence, and resistance to Babesia microti in male mice. *Physiology & Behavior.* **60**, 1223-1231 (1996).

15. Gaskill, B. N. et al. *Heat or Insulation: Behavioral Titration of Mouse Preference for Warmth or Access to a Nest. PLoS ONE.* **7**, e32799 (2012).

16. Sherwin, C. M., Haug, E., Terkelsen, N. & Vadgama, M. Studies on the motivation for burrowing by laboratory mice. *Applied Animal Behaviour Science.* **88**, 343-358 (2004).

17. Olsson, I. A. S. et al. Understanding behaviour: The relevance of ethological approaches in laboratory animal science. *Applied Animal Behaviour Science.* **81**, 245-264 (2003).

18. Holy, T. E. & Guo, Z. S. *Ultrasonic songs of male mice. PLoS Biology.* **3**, 2177-2186 (2005).

19. Arakawa, H., Cruz, S. & Deak, T. From models to mechanisms: Odorant communication as a key determinant of social behavior in rodents during illness-associated states. *Neuroscience and Biobehavioral Reviews.* **35**, 1916-1928 (2011).

20. Woolsey, T. A. & Vanderlo, H. Structural organization of layer-IV in somatosensory region (SI) of mouse cerebral cortex. Description of a cortical field composed of discrete cytoarchitectonic units. *Brain Research.* **17**, 205-242 (1970).

21. Cybulska-Klosowicz, A. & Kossut, M. Mice can learn roughness discrimination with vibrissae in a jump stand apparatus. *Acta Neurobiologiae Experimentalis.* **61**, 73-76 (2001).

22. Garner, J. P. et al. Animal neuropsychology: validation of the intra-dimensional extra-dimensional set shifting task for mice. *Behavioural Brain Research.* **173**, 53-61 (2006).

23. Mackintosh, J. Factors affecting the recognition of territory boundaries by mice (Mus musculus). *Animal Behaviour.* **21**, 464-470 (1973).

24. Brown, R. E. & Wong, A. A. The influence of visual ability on learning and memory performance in 13 strains of mice. *Learning and Memory.* **14**, 134-144 (2007).

25. Boissy, A. et al. Assessment of positive emotions in animals to improve their welfare. *Physiology & Behavior.* **92**, 375-397 (2007).

26. Held, S. D. E. & Špinka, M. Animal play and animal welfare. *Animal Behaviour.* **81**, 891-899 (2011).

27. Panksepp, J. The ontogeny of play in rats. *Developmental Psychobiology.* **14**, 327-332 (1981).

28. Webber, E. S. et al. Selective breeding for 50 kHz ultrasonic vocalization emission produces alterations in the ontogeny and regulation of rough-and-tumble play. *Behavioural Brain Research.* **229**, 138-144 (2012).

29. Pellis, S. & Pellis, V. *The playful brain.* (Oneworld, 2012).

30. Hess, S. E. et al. Home improvement: C57BL/6J mice given more naturalistic nesting materials make better nests. *Journal of the American Association for Laboratory Animal Science.* **47**, 25-31 (2008).

31. Nevison, C. M., Barnard, C. J. & Hurst, J. L. in *Paper presented at the 32nd International Congress of the International Society for Applied Ethology.* (Clermont-Ferrand, France, 1998).

32. Howerton, C. L., Garner, J. P. & Mench, J. A. Effects of running wheel-igloo enrichment on aggression, hierarchy linearity, and stereotypy in group-housed male CD-1 (ICR) mice. *Applied Animal Behaviour Science.* **115**, 90-103 (2008).

33. Van Loo, P. L. P. et al. Modulation of aggression in male mice: Influence of cage cleaning regime and scent marks. *Animal Welfare.* **9**, 281-295 (2000).

34. Gaskill, B. N. et al. Some like it hot: mouse temperature preferences in laboratory housing. *Applied Animal Behaviour Science.* **116**, 279-285 (2009).

35. Gaskill, B. N., Lucas, J. R., Pajor, E. A. & Garner, J. P. Working with what you've got: Changes in thermal preference and behavior in mice with or without nesting material. *Journal of Thermal Biology*. **36**, 1193-199 (2011).

36. Gaskill, B. N., Gordon, C. J., Pajor, E. A. & Garner, J. Impact of nesting material on mouse thermoregulation and variability. *Journal of the American Association for Laboratory Animal Science*. **48**, 549 (2009).

37. Gaskill, B. N., Garner, J. P. & Pritchett-Corning, K. R. Energy reallocation to breeding performance through improved behavioral thermoregulation. *Journal of the American Association for Laboratory Animal Science*. **50**, 771 (2011).

38. Mackintosh, N. J. in *Biology of the house mouse* (ed. Berry, R. J.). 337-366 (Academic Press, London, 1981).

39. Grant, E. C. & Mackintosh, J. H. A comparison of the social postures of some common laboratory rodents. *Behaviour*. **21**, 246-259 (1963).

40. Van Oortmerssen, G. A. Biological significance, genetics and evolutionary origin of variability in behaviour within and between inbred strains of mice (Mus musculus). *Behaviour*. **38**, 1-91 (1971).

41. Van Abeelen, J. H. F. Mouse mutants studied by means of ethological methods. 1. Ethogram. *Genetica*. **34**, 79-& (1963).

42. Martin, P. & Bateson, P. *Measuring behavior: an introductory guide.* (Cambridge University Press, Cambridge, 2004).

43. Young, R. J. *Environmental enrichment for captive animals* (eds. Kirkwood, J. K., Hubrecht, R. C. & Roberts, E. A.) (Blackwell Science Ltd, Oxford, 2003).

44. Bloomsmith, M. A., Brent, L. Y. & Schapiro, S. J. Guidelines for developing and managing an environmental enrichment program for nonhuman primates. *Laboratory Animal Science*. **41**, 372-377 (1991).

45. Humphrey, N. K. in *Growing Points in Ethology* (eds. Bateson, P. P. G. & Hinde, R. A.). 303-317 (Cambridge University Press, Cambridge, 1976).

46. Sharp, J., Zammit, T., Azar, T. & Lawson, D. Stress-like responses to common procedures in individually and group-housed female rats. *Contemporary Topics in Laboratory Animal Science*. **42**, 9-18 (2003).

47. Sharp, J. L., Zammit, T. G., Azar, T. A. & Lawson, D. M. Stress-like responses to common procedures in male rats housed alone or with other rats. *Contemporary Topics in Laboratory Animal Science*. **41**, 8-14 (2002).

48. Olsson, I. A. S. & Westlund, K. More than numbers matter: The effect of social factors on behaviour and welfare of laboratory rodents and non-human primates. *Applied Animal Behaviour Science*. **103**, 229-254 (2007).

49. Gonder, J. C. & Laber, K. A renewed look at laboratory rodent housing and management. *Ilar Journal*. **48**, 29-36 (2007).

50. Olsson, I. A. S. & Dahlborn, K. Improving housing conditions for laboratory mice: a review of environmental enrichment. *Laboratory Animals*. **36**, 243-270 (2002).

51. Van de Weerd, H. A. et al. Strength of preference for nesting material as environmental enrichment for laboratory mice. *Applied Animal Behaviour Science*. **55**, 369-382 (1998).

52. Roper, T. J. Nesting material as a reinforcer for female mice. *Animal Behaviour*. **21**, 733-740 (1973).

53. Lee, C. T. Genetic analysis of nest building behavior in laboratory mice (Mus-musculus). *Behavior Genetics*. **3**, 247-256 (1973).

54. Lee, C. T. & Wong, P. T. P. Temperature effect and strain differences in the nest-building behavior of inbred mice. *Psychonomic Science*. **20**, 9 (1970).

55. Lynch, C. B. Response to divergent selection for nesting behavior in Mus musculus. *Genetics*. **96**, 757-765 (1980).

56. Lynch, C. B. & Hegmann, J. P. Genetic differences influencing behavioral temperature regulation in small mammals. I. Nesting by *Mus musculus. Behavior Genetics*. **2**, 43-53 (1972).

57. Lynch, C. B. & Hegmann, J. P. Genetic differences influencing behavioral temperature regulation in small mammals. II. Genotype-environment interactions. *Behavior Genetics*. **3**, 145-154 (1973).

58. Gaskill, B. N. et al. Impact of nesting material on mouse body temperature and physiology. *Physiology & Behavior*. (in press).

59. Gaskill, B. N., Winnicker, C., Garner, J. P. & Pritchett-Corning, K. R. The naked truth: breeding performance in outbred and inbred strains of nude mice with and without nesting material. *Journal of the American Association for Laboratory Animal Science*. **50**, 741 (2011).

60. Breegi, S. Evaluation of nesting materials for use in nude mouse colonies. *Journal of the American Association for Laboratory Animal Science*. **50**, 782-782 (2011).

61. Van de Weerd, H. A. et al. Preferences for nesting material as environmental enrichments for laboratory mice. *Laboratory Animals*. **31**, 133-143 (1997).

62. Kaliste, E. K., Mering, S. M. & Huuskonen, H. K. Environmental modification and agonistic behavior in NIH/S male mice: Nesting material enhances fighting but shelters prevent it. *Comparative Medicine*. **56**, 202-208 (2006).

63. Gaskill, B. N., Rodda, C. & Garner, J. P. in *Paper presented at the International Behavioral Neuroscience Society 18th Annual Meeting*. (Nassau, Bahamas, 2009).

64. Lee, C. T. Development of nest-building behavior in inbred mice. *Journal of General Psychology*. **87**, 13 (1972).

65. Bazille, P. G., Walden, S. D., Koniar, B. L. & Gunther, R. Commercial cotton nesting material as a predisposing factor for conjunctivitis in athymic nude mice. *Lab Animal*. **30**, 40-42 (2001).

66. Rowson, K. E. K. & Michaels, L. Injury to young mice caused by cottonwool used as nesting material. *Laboratory Animals*. **14**, 187-187 (1980).

67. Macdonald, D. W. et al. Arable habitat use by wood mice (Apodemus sylvaticus). 3. A farm-scale experiment on the effects of crop rotation. *Journal of Zoology.* **250**, 313-320 (2000).

68. DeLong, K. T. Population Ecology of Feral House Mice. *Ecology.* **48**, 611-634 (1967).

69. Swetter, B. J., Karpiak, C. P. & Cannon, J. T. Separating the effects of shelter from additional cage enhancements for group-housed BALB/cJ mice. *Neuroscience Letters.* **495**, 205-209 (2011).

70. Pawlowicz, A., Demner, A. & Lewis, M. H. Effects of access to voluntary wheel running on the development of stereotypy. *Behavioural Processes.* **83**, 242-246 (2010).

71. Banjanin, S. & Mrosovsky, N. Preferences of mice, Mus musculus, for different types of running wheels. *Laboratory Animals.* **34**, 313-318 (2000).

72. Gordon, C. J. Effect of cage bedding on temperature regulation and metabolism of group-housed female mice. *Comparative Medicine.* **54**, 51-56 (2004).

73. Würbel, H., Chapman, R. & Rutland, C. Effect of feed and environmental enrichment on development of stereotypic wire-gnawing in laboratory mice. *Applied Animal Behaviour Science.* **60**, 69-81 (1998).

74. Whittaker, A. L., Howarth, G. S. & Hickman, D. L. Effects of space allocation and housing density on measures of well-being in laboratory mice: a review. *Laboratory Animals* (London). **46**, 3-13 (2012).

75. Van Loo, P. L. P. et al. Modulation of aggression in male mice: influence of group size and cage size. *Physiology & Behavior.* **72**, 675-683 (2001).

76. Kingston, S. G. & HoffmanGoetz, L. Effect of environmental enrichment and housing density on immune system reactivity to acute exercise stress. *Physiology & Behavior.* **60**, 145-150 (1996).

77. Cao, L. et al. Environmental and Genetic Activation of a Brain-Adipocyte BDNF/Leptin Axis Causes Cancer Remission and Inhibition. *Cell*. **142**, 52-64 (2010).

78. Morgan, K. N. & Tromborg, C. T. Sources of stress in captivity. *Applied Animal Behaviour Science*. **102**, 262-302 (2007).

79. Kempermann, G., Kuhn, H. G. & Gage, F. H. More hippocampal neurons in adult mice living in an enriched environment. *Nature*. **386**, 493-495 (1997).

80. Hurst, J. L. & West, R. S. Taming anxiety in laboratory mice. *Nat. Meth*. **7**, 825-826 (2010).

81. Nevison, C. M., Hurst, J. L. & Barnard, C. J. Why do male ICR(CD-1) mice perform bar-related (stereotypic) behaviour? *Behavioural Processes*. **47**, 95-111 (1999).

82. Phillips, K. A. et al. Double-mouse perch designed as an enrichment and life-saving device. *Journal of the American Association for Laboratory Animal Science*. **47**, 130-131 (2008).

83. Deacon, R. M. J. Digging and marble burying in mice: simple methods for *in vivo* identification of biological impacts. *Nature Protocols*. **1**, 122-124 (2006).

84. Berton, F., Vogel, E. & Belzung, C. Modulation of mice anxiety in response to cat odor as a consequence of predators diet. *Physiology & Behavior*. **65**, 247-254 (1998).

85. Blanchard, R. J., Yudko, E. B., Rodgers, R. J. & Blanchard, D. C. Defense system psychopharmacology — An ethological approach to the pharmacology of fear and anxiety. *Behavioural Brain Research*. **58**, 155-165 (1993).

86. Desjardins, C., Maruniak, J. A. & Bronson, F. H. Social rank in house mice: Differentiation revealed by ultraviolet visualization of urinary marking patterns. *Science*. **182**, 939-941 (1973).

87. Arakawa, H. et al. Scent marking behavior as an odorant communication in mice. *Neruoscience and Biobehavioral Reviews*. **32**, 1236-1248 (2008).

88. Morton, D. B. in *The ethology of domestic animals* (ed. Jensen, P.). (CABI, Oxford, 2002).

PART 3

Rat Behavior and Enrichment

Natural History & Behavior

The genus *Rattus* first emerged within the Muridae family about 3.5[1] to 5.6[2] million years ago, originating in Asia before spreading across the world.[3] The brown or Norway rat (*Rattus norvegicus*) settled in areas associated with human migration,[4] though exactly when they became commensal with humans is unclear. It is believed that the Norway rat was the first mammalian species domesticated primarily for scientific purposes.[3] Since the domesticated laboratory rat is descended from the Norway rat,[6,7] we will focus on the behavior of this species.

The home range of the wild Norway rat has been measured between 10 and 8,000 square meters, and not only are they able climbers,[7,8] but they build very elaborate burrow systems. The burrows of the wild Norway rat consist of tunnels averaging only 7.5 centimeters in height that connect chambers with an average height of 14.5 centimeters and go as deep as 3 meters.[5,9] Entries are generally located near a vertical wall or under a horizontal surface to allow for thigmotaxis.[9] Norway rats commonly burrow near water and are accomplished swimmers, with the ability to float up to 72 hours.[5]

In their burrows, rats live in large colonies of hundreds of animals.[7] The colonies consist of breeding demes, made up of females, males, and their subadult offspring.[10,11,12] Wild and feral (i.e., re-released domesticated) rats are polygamous, with the possibility of several males producing offspring in the same litter.[13] The rat's social structure consists of a dominance hierarchy in which fighting is essentially territorial, rather than to protect or secure the use of any specific resource.[9,14,15] At higher population densities, however, the social structure becomes despotic, where one rat is dominant and others are subordinate and a single male dominates the burrow system, keeping away most other males.[12,16,17]

While rats are considered nocturnal or crepuscular, they are observed to be active both during the day and at night.[9] However, since they tend to be active in low-light environments like dawn, dusk, or in burrows, they do not rely heavily on vision as a sense. Rats have a wider field of view, less binocular overlap, and much less acuity of vision than humans.[18] For rats, scent is the primary sense for monitoring their environment.[19] They relay information through their urine[20,21,22,23] and can discern gender, reproductive status, relatedness, dominance and alarm through scent markings.[24,25,26,27] Rats hear frequencies well into the ultrasonic, but their hearing range also overlaps with humans.[28] They produce a range of ultrasonic vocalizations, including 22 kilohertz vocalizations in response to aversive stimuli and 50 kilohertz vocalizations in association with positive affective states.[29,30,31] Touch is another sense that rats rely on heavily, particularly in order to navigate dark burrows and keep their bearings during nocturnal activity. Cortical areas in the brain devoted to the vibrissae (whiskers), nose and forepaws are enlarged compared to other areas of the body.[32] This indicates the high amount of sensory information being gathered from these areas of the body. During exploration, the whiskers are swept back and forth to identify obstacles, objects or food.[32,33]

Young rats are observed to spend much of their time engaged in social play (*Figure 1*). If housed in isolation during this critical period, abnormal patterns of social, sexual, and aggressive behaviors develop.[34] The degree to which rough and tumble play contributes to the development of dominant or aggressive behaviors, which are oriented towards the flank or sex organs, is unclear. Play may be more integral to the development of mating behaviors which, more like play, involve interactions centered around the head and scruff.[35] Additionally, when rats play they emit 50 kilohertz vocalizations, which, as mentioned previously, are associated with a positive affective state.[34] Thus, it is the opinion of the authors that play behavior is a pleasurable activity for rats, and potentially related to the development of later mating behaviors rather than aggression.

**For a video on rats engaging in playful behavior,
visit www.criver.com/behavior**

Figure 1: Rats at play. Reproduced with permission from Pellis, S. M. & Pellis, V. C., 1987.[35]

Behavior in the Laboratory

In the laboratory, rats are social and choose to retain contact with their conspecifics. Adult rats are often observed lying together or grooming each other[7] and will lever-press more often for access to familiar rats than for either novel objects or a larger cage.[12] Laboratory rats have been selected for many generations for tameness so that they are less fearful of humans and are more easily handled.[7] Incidentally, laboratory rats are more curious and less fearful of new objects than their wild counterparts.[7] Laboratory rats do display both territorial and dominance aggression; however, most encounters end in retreat or submission postures.[7] While many similarities with wild Norway rats have been conserved, laboratory rats have lost their aggressiveness towards humans as well as some of their fear of new objects in familiar environments.[7]

Observing and Quantifying Behavior

Basic Ethogram

A simple experimental ethogram, such as the one adapted from Abou-Ismail et al.[36] (*Table 1*), can be used to determine a rat's behavioral time budget. This ethogram covers different types of general activity, sleep, social interaction, aggression, and enrichment-directed behaviors. This can easily be used to determine if some change to the rat's environment, whether a new enrichment or change to the social structure, affects their behavior and potentially their welfare. Increasing amounts of play behavior in rats is considered to be a measure of positive welfare and would potentially be a good addition to the ethogram.[37] A more in-depth ethogram with detailed descriptions of behaviors can be found at www.ratbehavior.org or in the illustrated ethogram by Grant and Mackintosh.[38]

Rats, like many other rodents, secrete porphyrin from the Harderian gland near the eye.[39] High levels of secretion lead to chromodacryorrhea, or bloody tears, seen around the nose or eyes and is considered a sign of stress.[40,41] Mason et al.[40] developed and validated a scoring system for quantifying chromodacryorrhea in the laboratory as a measure of rat welfare. In the study, rats showed the highest amount of secretions due to building maintenance work, less to being exposed to an unfamiliar human, and even less if they were the subordinate animal in the group. Additionally, higher levels of chromodacryorrhea secretions have been found in rats just prior to cage cleaning, indicating that they find soiled bedding stressful.[41]

Table 1: Ethogram for Behavioral Elements Recorded

Category	Behavior
General Activity	Feeding or drinking Grooming or stretching Locomotion Exploratory behaviors Bedding directed behavior
Sleep	Sleep
Non-aggressive Social Interaction	
Agonism	Aggression Submission
Enrichment Oriented	
Other or Unknown	

Adapted from Abou-Ismail, V. A. et al., 2008.[36]

Description

Eating food from a hopper or drinking water from bottle sipper
Self-grooming, stretching or yawning
All locomotive behavior including climbing on the cage lid
Sniffing the cage floor, lid, or walls
Manipulation of bedding or nesting material

Lying motionless with the eyes closed

Social investigation, such as sniffing, and allogrooming
(includes the animal grooming and being groomed)

The rat is positioned over the other with its forepaws on the
subordinate rat
On-back posture exposing its ventral surface to the dominant rat

The manipulation of or interaction with the newly introduced
enrichment item. This may include chewing, sniffing or climbing

This includes any other behavior not listed above or if the animal
cannot be directly observed due to other animals or objects
in the cage

Behavioral Management

The use of choice or preference testing in the development of a behavioral husbandry strategy for rats can be challenging. Rats are highly adaptive, making it difficult to describe an "ideal" environment for them.[42] In addition, preferences are fluid: particular rewards often have different values in different situations or may vary with an animal's physiologic condition. For example, a food-deprived rat may choose food over nesting material, whereas a well-fed rat may choose differently.

Rats raised in a more naturalistic tunnel or underground housing system were found to be more reactive to laboratory events than those raised above ground.[43] This would suggest that keeping laboratory rats in a naturalistic environment is likely to stress them, as acclimation to human handling and research procedures is important for these animals.

With frequent, gentle handling, rats will become docile and easy to handle. Initial handling attempts must not involve negative stimuli, or the gentling becomes difficult or impossible. Making the animals easier to handle through habitations prior to study start can decrease stress or risk of injury to both animal and handler. Rats will learn an operant task to obtain gentle contact with a human as a reward.[44] Engaging rats with rapid finger movements across the nape of the neck and ventrum, mimicking play behavior (termed "tickling"), elicits 50 kilohertz vocalizations in rats normally associated with positive affective response. This technique has been shown to decrease the aversiveness that results from repeated IP injections.[45]

Enrichment

Social: For social species like the rat, social partners are the best enrichment because they are complex, novel and valued. In one study, Wistar rats housed in pairs or trios showed reduced stereotypic behaviors compared to singly-housed animals.[11,46]

Occupational:

• Burrowing substrate: Although burrowing is one of the most characteristic behaviors of the wild Norway rat, there is little work published on providing burrowing substrate to laboratory rats.

This is likely due to the practicality of providing and cleaning cages with burrowing substrate. The behavioral need to burrow appears to be increased during pregnancy,[9] thus behavioral frustration is likely increased in breeding females. However, considering that at least one study[43] found that rats raised in a naturalistic tunnel were less tame to laboratory events, this may not be a viable enrichment option.

• Nesting materials: Wild rat nest sites generally are found under overhead cover or within the burrow.[7] Although not preferred over a shelter, male and female laboratory rats do build nests;[43,47,48] however, strain differences in building are apparent. The motivation to engage in nest building is increased near parturition,[5] and is also affected by temperature.[7] Again, the lack of provision of material for this goal-directed behavior may be behaviorally frustrating to breeding females. While nest building is an innate behavior, there appears to be a learning component to it.[47] Rats prefer long-fiber materials[49] and appear to ignore soft paper shavings, wood shavings, and compressed cotton. Rats were found to eat tissues, especially if they were not exposed to them at an early age.[50] Rats provided crinkled paper (*Figures 3, 4 and 5*), built deeper nests than with tissue, soiled nests less, and were not seen to eat the material.[50] Paper strips were also found to be preferred over corn by-product

Figure 3: Rat nest built with crinkled paper nesting material. Charles River, 2012.

Figure 4: Crinkled paper rat nest. Note how the crinkled paper allows the rats to build a more complex, complete near-dome structure. Charles River, 2012.

Figure 5: Top view, crinkled paper rat nest. Charles River, 2012.

material.[51] Providing nesting material to rats, while not an ideal material to meet a rat's behavioral need to burrow, is likely the most practical and best occupational enrichment that can be provided to rats in the laboratory.

• Foraging: When foraging devices are available, rats generally spend less time feeding and more time searching for food.[52,53,54] Even though rats may spend less time feeding, if the meal found is large, rats may actually consume more food than from a traditional hopper.[52] Johnson et al.[52] hid food pellets in a shallow pan with gravel in the home cage to stimulate foraging behavior. This device was found to increase the occurrence of foraging and feeding behaviors not frequently seen in standard caging, such as searching, carrying food to a preferred location, and eating the pellet with the paws. A general preference test also showed the location with the foraging device to be preferred over other feeding or gnawing locations.

• Running wheels: Provision of running wheels to laboratory rats as enrichment is not common, most likely due to space restrictions. However, Morris and Johnson[55] found that rats which ran more in a running wheel self-stimulated the reward center (lateral hypothalamus) of their brain less, potentially illustrating the mood-enhancing effects of exercise.

• Gnawing materials: Rats, like mice, have open-rooted teeth and a need to gnaw. Laboratory rats on average spend six percent of their active period gnawing when substrates are available.[52] Multiple items are available for gnawing in rodents, including wood and nylon options. Wooden gnawing blocks have been found to reduce stereotypic wire gnawing on cage lids.[56] A study by Watson[57] found no significant differences in biochemical or hematologic values and no consistent effects in body weight or food consumption values between control and animals with nylon gnawing devices.

Physical environment:

• Enclosure:

   i. Size: Ideal housing densities for rats have yet to be confidently determined, likely due to their highly adaptable nature. Although data is conflicting, rats have been shown to prefer larger cages, whether in isolation or with conspecifics.[58] However, one study did show increased sleep disruption at higher stocking densities.[59] The value of increased space may not be as highly valued as increased complexity to rats;[6] however, increased cage size and complexity may go hand in hand, as increased complexity may require more space so that the devices do not crowd the animals.

ii. Complexity: It is possible that the welfare benefits of enrichment come from an increased complexity in the environment, and that the effect of a varied, complex environment is more influential than any one particular enrichment item. A recent study tested the hypothesis that a complex enriched environment would result in behaviors associated with increased welfare.[60] Despite not controlling for the number of objects provided, the study did support the hypothesis that providing multiple items in the cage increased the welfare indicators observed.

- Accessories:

i. Shelters or nest boxes: As a thigmotactic prey species often preyed upon from above, rats have shown preference for shelters over nesting material.[61,62] Opaque or semi-opaque structures were preferred.[49,63] When given the options, they will move nesting material into the shelter, making both shelters and nesting material viable enrichment options for rats.[61] In addition, the provision of a nest box has been observed to decrease the occurrence of stereotypic behavior, further supporting it as an enrichment that improves welfare.[64] Thus nest boxes, optimally paired with a nesting material, are likely to be the best enrichment items that can be provided to rats (based on the current literature).

ii. Tunnels or tubes: Conflicting evidence exists on the preference of tubes by rats.[65] Even though results are not straightforward, smaller laboratory rats have been observed to use PVC pipes more frequently than their larger conspecifics, suggesting that they may be escaping their dominant cage mate.[66]

iii. Climbing structures: Since the Norway rat is such an accomplished climber, vertical climbing structures are likely to be enriching. A cage with a wooden platform has been shown to be preferred over a standard cage, but was not preferred over nesting materials, suggesting that while structural complexity may be preferred over a simple environment, other enrichments may be of higher value.[67]

iv. Toys: In a review of environmental enrichment, it was mentioned that ping-pong balls were effective enrichments for young rats in toxicology studies.[68] As toys often do not meet any behavioral need or help rats reach any behavioral goal, it is unlikely that this is an effective enrichment. Interactions with an object are often misidentified as "play" and could potentially be fearful behavior.[69] Therefore it is recommended to provide rats with one of the aforementioned items that are behaviorally relevant, rather than balls, marbles or rattles.

Sensory: Providing enrichments that target the rat's primary senses, such as smell or touch, has the potential to be enriching, especially if learning is involved. However, no work has been conducted on this kind of environmental enrichment. Caution should be taken when providing smells. Adding scents to the home cage could potentially increase aggressive interactions, stress or behavioral frustration.

Nutritional:

• Delivery: The delivery of any type of highly valued item is extremely important. Care should be taken to make sure that both dominant and subordinate animals can gain access to and utilize provided enrichments. Additional care should be taken in rats since they are known to hoard food[7] and dominant animals may collect and guard food caches.

• Type: Rats are omnivorous, eating a wide range of foods and favoring those that are highly palatable.[7,70] Providing rats with different tastes, textures, and smells through a variety of foods is likely to be enriching.[71] Different food sources may require different food processing behaviors before being eaten, which will increase the behavioral complexity of captive rats. There are many options available for nutritional enrichment of rats, such as seeds, fruits or vegetables, and processed fruity pellets or gel treats.

Recommended Behavioral Husbandry Program

Based on the discussion above, it is likely that rats would benefit from the provision of gnawing and nesting materials, as well as a more complex home cage environment. Running wheels or the availability of multiple levels for exploration are potential means of increasing cage complexity. The provision of a shelter or nest box that provides both a hiding space to enter and an elevated flat platform suitable for climbing and resting on, particularly in conjunction with nesting material, would also likely be enriching. Providing rats with foraging opportunities can prove beneficial as well; however, more work should be done to explore this possibility. Rats are a social species, and social housing should be provided whenever compatible with scientific endpoints. While rats do engage in social play, it has not been shown that they engage in play with objects, so objects such as marbles or rattles are not recommended. An acclimation and handling program would be of benefit for rats, as they are highly adaptable and readily acclimate to human handling and research procedures.

References

1. Furano, A. V. & Usdin, K. DNA fossils and phylogenetic analysis — Using L1 (LINE-1, long interspersed repeated) DNA to determine the evolutionary history of mammals. *Journal of Biological Chemistry.* **270**, 25301-25304 (1995).

2. Verneau, O., Catzeflis, F. & Furano, A. V. Determining and dating recent rodent speciation events by using L1 (LINE-1) retrotransposons. *Proceedings of the National Academy of Sciences of the United States of America.* **95**, 11284-11289, doi:10.1073/pnas.95.19.11284 (1998).

3. Krinke, G. J. *The laboratory rat.* (Academic Press Inc., 2000).

4. Yoshida, T. H. *Cytogenetics of the black rat.* (University of Tokyo Press, 1980).

5. Meehan, A. P. *Rats and mice: Their biology and control.* (Brown Knight and Truscott Ltd, 1984).

6. Kaliste, E. & Mering, S., "The welfare of laboratory rats" in *The Welfare of Laboratory Animals* (ed. Kaliste, E.). 153-180 (Springer, 2007).

7. Barnett, S. A. *The rat: A study in behavior.* (University of Chicago Press, 1963).

8. Jackson, W. B. in *Wild mammals of North America* (eds. Chapman, J. A. & Feldhamer, G. A.). 1077-1088 (The Johns Hopkins University Press, 1982).

9. Calhoun, J. B. *The ecology and sociology of the Norway rat.* (U.S. Department of Health, Education, and Welfare, 1962).

10. Hurst, J. L. et al. Housing and welfare in laboratory rats: time-budgeting and pathophysiology in single-sex groups. *Animal Behavior.* **52**, 225-360 (1996).

11. Hurst, J. L., Barnard, C. J., Nevison, C. M. & West, C. D. Housing and welfare in laboratory rats: Welfare implications of isolation and social contact among caged males. *Animal Welfare.* **6**, 329-347 (1997).

12. Patterson-Kane, E. G., Hunt, M. & Harper, D. Rats Demand Social Contact. *Animal Welfare*. **11**, 327-332 (2002).

13. Berdoy, M. *The laboratory rat: A natural history*. <www.ratlife.org> (2003).

14. Blanchard, R. J., Flannelly, K. J. & Blanchard, D. C. Life-span studies of dominance and aggression in established colonies of laboratory rats. *Physiology & Behavior*. **43**, 1-7 (1988).

15. Blanchard, D. C. et al. Dominance and aggression in social groups of male and female rats. *Behavioural Processes*. **9**, 31-48 (1984).

16. Hurst, J. L. et al. Housing and welfare in laboratory rats: time-budgeting and pathophysiology in single-sex groups. *Animal Behaviour*. **52**, 335-360 (1996).

17. Lott, D. F. Intraspecific Variation in the Social Systems of Wild Vertebrates. *Behaviour*. **88**, 266-325 (1984).

18. Burn, C. C. What is it like to be a rat? Rat sensory perception and its implications for experimental design and rat welfare. *Appl. Anim. Behav. Sci.* **112**, 1-32, doi:10.1016/j.applanim.2008.02.007 (2008).

19. Kemppinen, N. M. et al. The Effect of Dividing Walls, a Tunnel, and Restricted Feeding on Cardiovascular Responses to Cage Change and Gavage in Rats (Rattus norvegicus). *Journal of the American Association for Laboratory Animal Science*. **48**, 157-165 (2009).

20. Mackay-Sim, A. & Laing, D. G. The sources of odors from stressed rats. *Physiology & Behavior*. **27**, 511-513 (1981).

21. Abel, E. L. & Bilitzke, P. J. A possible alarm substance in the forced swimming test. *Physiology & Behavior*. **48**, 233-239 (1990).

22. Williams, J. L. & Groux, M. L. Exposure to various stressors alters preferences for natural odors in rats (*Rattus norvegicus*). *Journal of Comparative Psychology*. **107**, 39-47 (1993).

23. Kiyokawa, Y., Kikusui, T., Takeuchi, Y. & Mori, Y. Modulatory role of testosterone in alarm pheromone release by male rats. *Hormones and Behavior*. **45**, 122-127 (2004).

24. Alberts, J. R. & Galef, B. G. Olfactory cues and movement: stimuli mediating intraspecific aggression in the wild Norway rat. *Journal of Comparative Physiological Psychology*. **85**, 233-242 (1973).

25. Moore, C. L. Sex differences in urinary odors produced by young laboratory rats (Rattus norvegicus). *Journal of Comparative Psychology*. **99**, 336-341 (1985).

26. Brown, R. E. Responses of dominant and subordinate male-rats to the odors of male and female conspecifics. *Aggressive Behavior*. **18**, 129-138 (1992).

27. Garcia-Brull, P. D., Nunez, J. & Nunez, A. The effect of scents on the territorial and aggressive-behavior of laboratory rats. *Behavioral Processess*. **29**, 25-36 (1993).

28. Heffner, H. E. & Heffner, R. S. Hearing ranges of laboratory animals. *Journal of the American Association for Laboratory Animal Science*. **46**, 11-13 (2007).

29. Portfors, C. V. Types and functions of ultrasonic vocalizations in laboratory rats and mice. *J. Am. Assoc. Lab. Anim. Sci.* **46**, 28-34 (2007).

30. Wintink, A. J. & Brudzynski, S. M. The related roles of dopamine and glutamate in the initiation of 50-kHz ultrasonic calls in adult rats. *Pharmacology Biochemistry and Behavior*. **70**, 317-323 (2001).

31. Burgdorf, J. & Panksepp, J. Tickling induces reward in adolescent rats. *Physiology and Behavior*. **72**, 167-173 (2001).

32. Whishaw, I. Q. & Kolb, B. *The behavior of the laboratory rat.* (Oxford University Press, 2004).

33. Mitchinson, B. et al. Active vibrissal sensing in rodents and marsupials. *Philosophical Transactions of the Royal Society B: Biological Sciences*. **366**, 3037-3048, doi:10.1098/rstb.2011.0156 (2011).

34. Vanderschuren, L., Niesink, R. J. M. & VanRee, J. M. The neurobiology of social play behavior in rats. *Neuroscience and Biobehavioral Reviews*. **21**, 309-326, doi:10.1016/s0149-7634(96)00020-6 (1997).

35. Pellis, S. M. & Pellis, V. C. Play-fighting differs from serious fighting in both target of attack and tactics of fighting in the laboratory rat *Rattus norvegicus*. *Aggressive Behav.* 13, 227-242, doi:10.1002/1098-2337(1987)13:4<227::aid-ab2480130406>3.0.co;2-c (1987).

36. Abou-Ismail, U. A., Burman, O. H. P., Nicol, C. J. & Mendl, M. Let sleeping rats lie: Does the timing of husbandry procedures affect laboratory rat behaviour, physiology and welfare? *Applied Animal Behaviour Science.* **111**, 329-341, doi:10.1016/j.applanim.2007.06.019 (2008).

37. Held, S. D. E. & Špinka, M. Animal play and animal welfare. *Animal Behaviour.* **81**, 891-899 (2011).

38. Grant, E. C. & Mackintosh, J. H. A comparison of the social postures of some common laboratory rodents. *Behaviour.* **21**, 246-259 (1963).

39. Buzzell, G. R. The harderian gland: Perspectives. *Microscopy Research and Technique.* **34**, 2-5 (1996).

40. Mason, G., Wilson, D., Hampton, C. & Wurbel, H. Non-invasively assessing disturbance and stress in laboratory rats by scoring chromodacryorrhoea. *Alternatives to laboratory Animals.* **32**, 153-159 (2004).

41. Burn, C. C., Peters, A. & Mason, G. J. Acute effects of cage cleaning at different frequencies on laboratory rat behaviour and welfare. *Anim. Welf.* **15**, 161-171 (2006).

42. Sorensen, D. B. et al. An ethological approach to housing requirements of golden hamsters, Mongolian gerbils and fat sand rats in the laboratory: A review. *Applied Animal Behaviour Science.* **94**, 181-195 (2005).

43. Boice, R. Burrows of wild and albino rats — Effects of domestication, outdoor raising, age, experience, and maternal state. *Journal of Comparative and Physiological Psychology.* **91**, 649-661, doi:10.1037/h0077338 (1977).

44. Davis, H. & Perusse, R. Human-based social interaction can reward a rat's behavior. *Learning & Behavior.* **16**, 89-92 (1988).

45. Cloutier, S., Wahl, K. & Newberry, R. C. Playful Handling Mitigates the Stressfulness of Injections in Laboratory Rats. *J. Am. Assoc. Lab. Anim. Sci.* **49**, 721-721 (2010).

46. Hurst, J. L., Barnard, C. J., Nevison, C. M. & West, C. D. Housing and welfare in laboratory rats: The welfare implications of social isolation and social contact among females. *Anim. Welf.* **7**, 121-136 (1998).

47. Jegstrup, I. M., Vestergaard, R., Vach, W. & Ritskes-Hoitinga, M. Nest-building behaviour in male rats from three inbred strains: BN/HsdCpb, BDIX/OrlIco and LEW/Mol. *Animal Welfare.* **14**, 149-156 (2005).

48. Blom, H. et al. Preferences of mice and rats for types of bedding material. *Laboratory Animals.* **30**, 234-244 (1996).

49. Manser, C. E., Broom, D. M., Overend, P. & Morris, T. H. Investigations into the preferences of laboratory rats for nest-boxes and nesting materials. *Lab. Anim.* **32**, 23-35, doi:10.1258/002367798780559365 (1998).

50. Van Loo, R. L. R. & Baumans, V. The importance of learning young: the use of nesting material in laboratory rats. *Laboratory Animals.* **38**, 17-24 (2004).

51. Ras, T., van de Ven, M., Patterson-Kane, E.G. & Nelson, K. Rats' preferences for corn versus wood-based bedding and nesting materials. *Laboratory Animals.* **36**, 420-425 (2002).

52. Johnson, S. R., Patterson-Kane, E. G. & Niel, L. Foraging enrichment for laboratory rats. *Animal Welfare.* **13**, 305-312 (2004).

53. Gannon, K. N., Smith, H. V. & Tiernet, K. J. Effect of procurement cost on food consumption in rats. *Physiology and Behavior.* **31**, 331-337 (1983).

54. Johnson, D. F., Ackroff, K. M., Collier, G. H. & Plescia, L. Effects of dietary nutrients and foraging cost on meal patterns of rats. *Physiology and Behavior.* **33**, 465-471 (1984).

55. Morris, M. J., Na, E. S. & Johnson, A. K. Voluntary Running-Wheel Exercise Decreases the Threshold for Rewarding Intracranial Self-Stimulation. *Behavioral Neuroscience.* **126**, 582-587, doi:10.1037/a0029149 (2012).

56. Orok-Edem, E. & Key, D. Responses of rats (Rattus norvegicus) to enrichment objects. *Animal Technology.* **45**, 25-30 (1994).

57. Watson, D. S. B. Evaluation of inanimate objects on commonly monitored variables in preclinical safety studies for mice and rats. *Lab. Anim. Sci.* **43**, 378-380 (1993).

58. Patterson-Kane, E. G. Cage Size Preference in Rats in the Laboratory. *Journal of Applied Animal Welfare Science.* **5**, 63-72 (2002).

59. Abou-Ismail, U. A., Burman, O. H. P., Nicol, C. J. & Mendl, M. Can sleep behaviour be used as an indicator of stress in group-housed rats (*Rattus norvegicus*)? *Anim. Welf.* **16**, 185-188 (2007).

60. Abou-Ismail, U. A. Are the effects of enrichment due to the presence of multiple items or a particular item in the cages of laboratory rat? *Appl. Anim. Behav. Sci.* **134**, 72-82 (2011).

61. Manser, C. E., Broom, D. M., Overend, P. & Morris, T. H. Operant studies to determine the strength of preference in laboratory rats for nest-boxes and nesting materials. *Lab. Anim.* **32**, 36-41, doi:10.1258/002367798780559473 (1998).

62. Patterson-Kane, E. C., Harper, D. N. & Hunt, M. The cage preferences of laboratory rats. *Lab. Anim.* **35**, 74-79, doi:10.1258/0023677011911390 (2001).

63. Olsson, I. A. S. et al. Understanding behaviour: The relevance of ethological approaches in laboratory animal science. *Appl. Anim. Behav. Sci.* **81,** 245-264 (2003).

64. Callard, M. D., Bursten, S. N. & Price, E. O. Repetitive backflipping behaviour in captive roof rats (Rattus rattus) and the effects of cage enrichment. *Animal Welfare.* **9**, 139-152 (2000).

65. Patterson-Kane, E. G. Enrichment of laboratory caging for rats: a review. *Animal Welfare.* **13**, S209-S214 (2004).

66. Galef, B. G., Sorge, R. E. Use of PVC Conduits by Rats of Various Strains and Ages Housed Singly and in Pairs. *Journal o. Applied Animal Welfare Science.* **3**, 279-292 (2000).

67. Bradshaw, A. L. & Poling, A. Choice by rats for enriched versus standard home cages: plastic pipes, wood platforms, wood chips, and paper towels as enrichment items. *Journal of the Experimental Analysis of Behavior*. **55**, 245-250 (1991).

68. Dean, S. W. Environmental enrichment of laboratory animals used in regulatory toxicology studies. *Laboratory Animals*. **33**, 309-327 (1999).

69. Deacon, R. M. J. Digging and marble burying in mice: simple methods for in vivo identification of biological impacts. *Nature Protocols*. **1**, 122-124 (2006).

70. Barnett, S. A. & Spencer, M. M. Experiments on the food preferences of wild rats (Rattus norvegicus berkenhout). *Journal of Hygiene*. **51**, 16-34 (1953).

71. Jennings, M. et al. Refining rodent husbandry: The mouse — Report of the Rodent Refinement Working Party. *Laboratory Animals*. **32**, 233-259 (1998).

Natural History & Behavior

Hamsters are terrestrial animals. Native to western Asia, their natural habitat is either dry, rocky plains or lightly vegetated slopes where resources are relatively scarce. The summer climate consists of hot and dry days, whereas winters can be wet and cool.[1,2] While nocturnal in the laboratory, hamsters in the wild have been observed to be diurnal,[3] leaving their burrows to forage for food, stuffing their cheek pouches and carrying what they find back to their burrows for hoarding. Their diet is varied, consisting mostly of grains, plant roots and shoots, insects and fruit.[4]

Hamsters dig burrows and will hibernate at low temperatures. True hibernators, they reduce their metabolic rate to conserve energy, and generally hibernate between November and February,[1] when temperatures drop to 5-19°C. Optimal conditions for hibernation include the availability of nesting material, enough food to establish a store, cooler temperatures and time (generally several weeks).

Similar to other rodents, hamsters distinguish individuals by scent left in urine, feces or flank gland secretions.[5] This ability to distinguish individuals is related to social order and the determination of dominance rank, as well as territory and resource marking. In nature, hamsters are solitary creatures and only come into contact for mating. Both males and females display territorial scent marking with their flank glands and territories are viciously defended against intruders. Female hamsters are larger and more aggressive than their male counterparts.[6] Dominance among females appears to be stable, linear and related to body weight and androgen levels.[7] Agonistic encounters, similar to other rodents, generally consist of dominance behavior displayed by one animal, responded to by submissive and retreat behaviors by the subordinate animal.

For a video on hamsters exhibiting dominance behavior, visit www.criver.com/behavior

Like mice and rats, hamsters communicate via ultrasonic vocalizations.[9] Both male and female hamsters emit sounds with dominant frequencies of 32-42 kilohertz, generally associated with mating behavior.[10] In one series of experiments, hamster calls were highly situation-dependent, suggesting a role in social communication. Both male and female calls were influenced by odor and estrous cycle stage, intimating that the communication system is involved in facilitating reproductive encounters.[10,11,12]

As a solitary species, female hamsters attract mates by leaving a vaginal scent trail when they are fertile. Their interactions with the males are aggressive during late estrus and early diestrus, but as their cycle proceeds, their aggressiveness wanes to receptive behaviors. This receptive period generally lasts only about a week surrounding mating.[13] The receptive female displays lordosis behavior, a posture of flattened back and elevated tail. Mating is brief and shortly followed by the female chasing the male from her nest site and retrieving his food supply for her own hoard.[14]

Figure 1: Hamster with pups in nest. Charles River, 2012

**For a video on a female hamster building a nest,
visit www.criver.com/behavior**

During the last third of gestation and the first week after birth, female hamsters increase nest building activities. Like other rodents, hamsters build nests in late gestation and when under cold stress.[15,16] Similar to other species that give birth to altricial young, pups are nursed and groomed intensely at first, with the activities and time in the nest tapering off nearing the 21st day post-birth[17] (*Figure 1*). Natural weaning occurs at about 3 ½ weeks of age, sexual maturity is reached by 42 days of age, and optimal reproductive age is reached by 8-10 weeks in females and 10-12 weeks in males.[4]

Adolescent hamsters play-fight starting at about 15 days old, increasing to a peak at about 35-40 days, then decreasing (or transitioning to actual fighting) with maturity.[18] Play fighting is characterized by tumbling and pinning, with no establishment o dominance. Contact and play is most vigorous between pups of similar age. It has been observed that isolation increases the amount of play fighting at first, which then tapers off over time.[19]

Behavior in the Laboratory

Laboratory hamsters are believed to have originated from a few founding animals that were littermates (Murphy, 1985, referenced by Sorensen et al., 2005).[2] Thus, there is little genetic diversity within the laboratory hamster population.

Provided with appropriate substrate, laboratory hamsters will build burrows just like their wild relatives. Each burrow generally contains only one female and her litter. The structure of the burrow generally consists of two tunnels off the nest chamber: one for toileting and one for food storage.[1] The nest chamber is generally found at a depth of about 50 centimeters.[1] The smallest observed distance between inhabited burrows in the wild was 118 millimeters in one observational study.[1]

Despite being a solitary species, most laboratory hamsters are group housed (*Figure 2*). It has been found that socially housed hamsters spend more time in social contact than not, particularly if the animals had prior social housing experience.[20] Prior experience plays a significant role in hamster behavior and therefore significantly influences behavioral management and enrichment of the species. Socially reared male hamsters show

Figure 2: Group housed hamsters. Charles River, 2012

submissive behaviors at closer distances than ones raised in isolation,[21] suggesting that an increased tolerance for social environments is something of a learned behavior. While there is an increased risk of injury from fighting, hamsters seem to prefer social housing.[2,20] It is likely that early housing experience affects later social preference and behavior in hamsters, and the social housing paradigms in production environments allow for a more social animal in laboratory-reared conditions.

Observing & Quantifying Behavior

In order to develop and assess a behavioral husbandry program, behavioral interventions must involve behavioral observation before and after implementation to determine the effect. An ethogram is a list of behaviors. Most of the time, however, a full ethogram is not required, and a research ethogram is developed that contains just the behaviors of interest for a particular experiment or behavioral intervention. For instance, if the aim of an enrichment or other behavioral intervention is to decrease aggression, then perhaps only aggressive and submissive behaviors would be documented. A well-developed ethogram, as described in other chapters (mouse and gerbil), tightly defines behaviors so that their observation is consistent in time and between observers.

Table 1: Examples of Potential Research Ethograms. Winnicker, 2012

Category	Behavior
Active	General locomotion
	Rearing
	Climbing
	Digging
	Marking
Maintenance	Grooming
	Feeding or drinking
	Food Hoarding
	Nest Building
Inactive	Sleeping/Resting
	Still and alert
Social	Attend
	Approach
	Body-sniff
	Social Groom

(continued on next page)

Adapted from multiple sources.[8,14,20,22,23]

Description

Horizontal locomotion: moving walking, running, creeping
Head raised, looking around, sniffing, also erect on hind legs
Vertical locomotion: clinging to or climbing on the wire, hind legs lifted
off the floor
Scraping with forepaws, ejecting material with hind legs; pushing
bedding material aside
Animal rubs its flank glands over an object or side of cage

All grooming behavior, including licking the fur, grooming with the
forepaws and scratching with any limb. Grooming is usually
performed in a sitting position with the animal's hindquarters
in contact with the floor; may only involve the vibrissae.
Eating, sniffing and/or gnawing at food, filling cheek pouches,
treating food with paws; drinking from the water spigot.
The carrying of food and piling in distinct locations
Carrying of nesting substrate to and piling in a distinct location

The animal is motionless or standing still, freezing movement for greater
than one second. Could be either lying curled up on its side or sitting
curled up, with its face tucked into its body and out of sight.
The animal is sitting or curled up but, in contrast to sleep, the face is
lifted. The animal either sits motionless, or appears to be orientating its
head to sounds outside of the cage.

Turning head towards conspecific
Animal moves toward conspecific following attend behavior; preempts
all aggressive/submissive interactions.
Sniffing another hamster's body
Oral or manual manipulation of another hamster, excluding tail-tugging
or biting

Table 1: Examples of Potential Research Ethograms. Winnicker, 2012 (continued)

Category	Behavior
Aggression	Threat
	Chase
	Attack
	Tumble/Fight
	Spar
Submissive	Evade/Retreat
	Freeze on back
	Defensive posture
Reproductive	Lordosis
	Tail up
	Prelordosis
	Mount

Adapted from multiple sources.[8,14,20,22,23]

Description

One hamster displays upright or sideways offensive postures, usually
followed by chase, attack, tumble/fight.
One hamster pursues another.
One hamster bites another.
Generally seen after chase, hamsters clap each other, rolling over and
over in rapid tumbling movements, often accompanied by vocalization
and biting; may be two or more hamsters.
Two hamsters standing on hind legs and "boxing" with their forepaws

One hamster runs from a pursuer.
Lying flat on back with extremities extended with conspecific either next
to or over them
Orienting with head bent away from another hamster, with forepaws
raised to cover the chest

Standing posture with the back flattened horizontally and the tail
elevated (female)
Standing or walking with the tail held vertically (male)
Standing or walking with the tail held vertically (female)
One animal mounts the other; irrelevant of orientation or intromission

Table 1 examples of potential research ethograms, grouped by type of behavior that could be usefully adapted in the development of a behavioral husbandry program for hamsters.

Behavioral Management

Enrichment

Solid-bottom caging allows for bedding that can accommodate natural digging, burrowing and nest-building behaviors. Hamsters have shown a preference for solid-bottom caging with bedding versus wire-bottom caging in spite of a reduction in floor space.[24] In addition, hamsters housed on pine shavings had less foot lesions than hamsters housed on beta chips, a smaller hardwood chip, indicating that this bedding type may result in better welfare.[25]

Hamsters generally show preference for enclosed or darkened areas. In one experiment, when provided with both mason jars and a PVC T-pipe, hamsters seemed to prefer the jar, perhaps because of its similarity in structure to natural burrows.[24] Given the option, hamsters will choose to build a nest in a darker nest box as opposed to a lighter one; additionally, they will choose the dark box over one with closer proximity to resources or a larger size.[26] Interestingly, in the same experiment, size prevailed over distance from resource, with hamsters preferentially choosing the larger nest box over the smaller one that was located closer to nesting material. In another study, shelters, semi-closed pipes, and open-ended pipes were offered to hamsters. If hamsters did not nest in the shelters, they frequently nested next to them, and the semi-closed pipe was preferred.[27] The semi-closed pipe structure is similar to the blind-end natural burrow that hamsters would build in the wild, perhaps explaining the preference. PVC tunnels have also been show to decrease the aggressive behavior of hamsters housed on wire caging,[28] another potential benefit to providing a tunnel or burrow-type structure.

Both male and female hamsters will build a nest in the laboratory (*Figure 3*). In one study, when given free access to straw nesting material, hamsters used from 15 to 25 grams of

Figure 3: Hamster nest material and food hoard. Charles River, 2012

material, building a larger nest when pregnant,[29] suggesting
that the volume of material provided for nest building should be
at least 15 grams, and potentially more for pregnant females.
Hamsters appear to prefer used nesting material to new, with
both males and females choosing to remain in nests that
had not been changed for up to 14 days, despite having new
nesting material readily available.[30] This suggests that hamsters
are not bothered by old nesting material and, in fact, prefer it.
The provision of nesting material has been shown to improve
the appetite and responsiveness of the animals.[28] Perhaps the
stress of cage changing could, at least in part, be mitigated by
the retention of material around the nest site in the new, clean
cage.

Hoarding is an important behavior in hamsters.[31] If food is only
provided via a food hopper, then the ability to collect and hoard
it in a store is lost. Overall, wild hamsters spend very little time
outside the burrow collecting food, likely influenced by exposure
risk. Lactating hamsters will spend significantly more time out
of the burrow, indicating that this is an energy need-driven
behavior.[32] Providing the food inside the cage, such as on the

**For a video on a hamster exhibiting natural hoarding
behavior, visit www.criver.com/behavior**

cage floor, allows the animals to display this natural hoarding behavior. Nesting material is also a hoarded resource. When provided with material, whether it be food or nesting substrate, the farther the material was located from the nest site, the less that was hoarded. This would suggest that distance from the main hoard and ease of transport are important factors in the determination of a material's hoardability.[26]

While not traditionally thought of as a social species, socially raised laboratory hamsters can generally coexist in a relatively peaceful manner in social laboratory housing. Early life experience appears to contribute to this social success,[21] and it is the experience of the authors that social housing is indeed possible when initiated at a young age.

Recommended Enrichment/Husbandry

Hamsters prefer solid-floor caging with bedding,[24] although prior experience can affect their preference. Since solid-floor caging with bedding allows for the ability to nest and hoard, it is behaviorally desirable for hamsters. This type of housing may also offer additional advantages. If provided with deep enough bedding, hamsters will burrow to a depth of 50 centimeters, similar to the depth of their naturally occurring burrows.[1,22] Hamsters also display less wire-gnawing and wheel-running activity when given enough bedding to burrow in, suggesting a better welfare state. In one study, 50 percent of hamsters with bedding 10 centimeters deep engaged in wire gnawing, whereas hamsters with bedding 80 centimeters deep did not.[22] In the same study, all hamsters were provided with a shelter, but these were ultimately utilized solely by the shallow-bedded group, and then only for resting; the deep-bedded group preferred to build and rest in their burrows. Even though hamsters provided with shelters will rest in them, when given the choice, they preferentially burrow.[22] While the ideal depth of bedding cannot be determined from the current body of work, it is clear that deeper bedding allows for burrowing and should be considered as preferential. Shelters or nest boxes may also provide some comfort when used with shallow bedding.[22]

As hamsters will nest-build and are behaviorally driven to create a hoard of both food and nest materials, both should be provided. Ideally, food and nesting material should be provided inside the cage so that the materials can be readily picked up and transported to the hoarding location by the animals.

Due to their nocturnal nature, hamsters awoken from their daytime sleep tend to be irritable. Thus, poking or prodding them awake from sleep for handling, procedures or cage change can elicit a bite response. Scooping or cupping the animals up with two hands renders them less likely to bite when being handled.[33]

Since laboratory-raised hamsters are socially housed in production environments, they have adapted behaviorally to social housing. As a result, it is likely that social housing is preferred in these animals. While there is some potential for fighting, the value of social contact to the animals is significant enough that the effort to implement social housing should be made.

References

1. Gattermann, R. et al. Notes on the current distribution and the ecology of wild golden hamsters (*Mesocricetus auratus*). *Journal of Zoology.* **254**, 359-365 (2001).

2. Sorensen, D. B. et al. An ethological approach to housing requirements of golden hamsters, Mongolian gerbils and fat sand rats in the laboratory — A review. *Applied Animal Behaviour Science.* **94**, 181-195 (2005).

3. Gattermann, R. et al. Golden hamsters are nocturnal in captivity but diurnal in nature. *Biology Letters.* **4**, 253-255 (2008).

4. Whittaker, D. *The UFAW Handbook on The Care and Management of Laboratory and Other Research Animals; The Syrian hamster* (eds. Hubrecht, R. & Kirkwood, J.). (Wiley-Blackwell, 2010).

5. Johnston, R. E. et al. Individual scent signatures in golden hamsters: evidence for specialization of function. *Animal Behaviour.* **45**, 1061-1070 (1993).

6. Grelk, D. F. et al. Influence of Caging Conditions and Hormone Treatments on Fighting in Male and Female Hamsters. *Hormones and Behavior.* **5**, 355-366 (1974).

7. Drickamer, L. C., Vangenbergh, J. G. & Colby, D. R. Predictors of social dominance in the adult female golden hamster (*Mesocricetus auratus*). *Animal Behaviour.* **21**, 564-570 (1973).

8. Lerwill, C. J. & Makings, P. Agonistic Behavior of Golden-Hamster *Mesocricetus auratus* (Waterhouse). *Animal Behaviour.* **19**, 714-721 (1971).

9. Cherry, J. A. Ultrasonic vocalizations by male hamsters: parameters of calling and effects of playbacks on female behaviour. *Animal Behaviour.* **38**, 138-153 (1989).

10. Floody, O. R. & Pfaff, D. W. Communication among hamsters by high-frequency acoustic signals: I. Physical characteristics of hamster calls. *Journal of Comparative and Physiological Psychology.* **91**, 794-806 (1977).

11. Floody, O. R. & Pfaff, D. W. Communication among hamsters by high-frequency acoustic signals: III. Response evoked by natural and synthetic ultrasounds. *Journal of Comparative and Physiological Psychology.* **91**, 820-829 (1977).

12. Floody, O. R., Pfaff, D. W. & Lewis, C. D. Communication among hamsters by high-frequency acoustic signals: II. Determinants of calling by females and males. *Journal of Comparative and Physiological Psychology.* **91**, 807-819 (1977).

13. Marques, D. M. & Valenstein, E. S. Individual-Differences in Aggressiveness of Female Hamsters — Response to Intact and Castrated Males and to Females. *Animal Behaviour.* **25**, 131-139 (1977).

14. Lisk, R. D., Ciaccio, L. A. & Catanzaro, C. Mating behaviour of the golden hamster under seminatural conditions. *Animal Behaviour.* **31**, 659-666 (1983).

15. Bhatia, A. J., Schneider, J. E. & Wade, G. N. Thermoregulatory and maternal nestbuilding in Syrian hamsters: Interaction of ovarian steroids and energy demand. *Physiology & Behavior.* **58**, 141-146 (1995).

16. Kauffman, A. S., Paul, M. J., Butler, M. P. & Zucker, I. Huddling, locomotor, and nest-building behaviors of furred and furless Siberian hamsters. *Physiology & Behavior.* **79**, 247-256 (2003).

17. Nichita, I., Seres, M. & Coman, C. Maternal Behaviour on Golden Hamster (*Mesocricetus auratus*). *Lucrari Stiintifice – Medicina Veterinara.* **XLIII**, 335-340 (2010).

18. Guerra, R. F., Vieira, M. L., Takase, E. & Gasparetto, S. Sex differences in the play fighting activity of golden hamster infants. *Physiology & Behavior.* **52**, 1-5 (1992).

19. Guerra, R. F., Takase, E. & Nunes, C. R. O. Play fighting of juvenile golden hamsters (*Mesocricetus auratus*): effects of two types of social deprivation and days of testing. *Behavioural Processes.* **47**, 139-151 (1999).

20. Arnold, C. E. & Estep, D. Q. Effects of housing on social preference and behaviour in male golden hamsters (*Mesocricetus auratus*). *Applied Animal Behaviour Science.* **27**, 253-261 (1990).

21. Huang, D. & Hazlett, B. A. Submissive Distance in Golden-Hamster *Mesocricetus-Auratus. Animal Behaviour.* **22**, 467-472 (1974).

22. Hauzenberger, A. R., Gebhardt-Henrich, S. G. & Steiger, A. The influence of bedding depth on behaviour in golden hamsters (*Mesocricetus auratus*). *Applied Animal Behaviour Science.* **100**, 280-294 (2006).

23. Payne, A. P. The aggressive response of the male golden hamster towards males and females of differing hormonal status. *Animal Behaviour.* **22**, Part 4, 829-835 (1974).

24. Arnold, C. E. & Estep, D. Q. Laboratory Caging Preferences in Golden-Hamsters (*Mesocricetus-Auratus*). *Laboratory Animals.* **28**, 232-238 (1994).

25. Beaulieu, A. & Reebs, S. G. Effects of bedding material and running wheel surface on paw wounds in male and female Syrian hamsters. *Laboratory Animals.* **43**, 85-90 (2009).

26. Ottoni, E. B. & Ades, C. Resource Location and Structural-Properties of the Nestbox as Determinants of Nest-Site Selection in the Golden-Hamster. *Animal Learning & Behavior.* **19**, 234-240 (1991).

27. Veillette, M. & Reebs, S. G. Shelter choice by Syrian hamsters (*Mesocricetus auratus*) in the laboratory. *Animal Welfare.* **20**, 603-611 (2011).

28. McClure, D. E. & Thomson, J. I. Cage enrichment for hamsters housed in suspended wire cages. *Contemporary Topics in Laboratory Animal Science.* **31**, 33 (1992).

29. Richards, M. P. Effects of Oestrogen and Progesterone on Nest Building in Golden Hamster. *Animal Behaviour.* **17**, 356-361 (1969).

30. Veillette, M. & Reebs, S. G. Preference of Syrian hamsters to nest in old versus new bedding. *Applied Animal Behaviour Science.* **125**, 189-194 (2010).

31. Guerra, R. F. & Ades, C. An analysis of travel costs on transport of load and nest building in golden hamster. *Behavioural Processes.* **57**, 7-28 (2002).

32. Larimer, S. C. et al. Foraging behavior of golden hamsters (*Mesocricetus auratus*) in the wild. *Journal of Ethology.* **29**, 275-283 (2011).

33. Kuhnen, G. in *Comfortable Quarters for Laboratory Animals* (eds. Reinhardt, V. & Reinhardt, A.). 33-37 (Animal Welfare Institute, Washington, 2002).

PART 5

Gerbil Behavior and Enrichment

Natural History & Behavior

Meriones unguiculatus,[1] commonly known as the Mongolian gerbil or the clawed jird, is a small rodent from the steppes of Asia. Gerbils are part of the Gerbillinae family, which comprises 103 gerbilline species in 16 genera.[2] These small rodents are root, seed and plant eaters, with one study showing the main portion of their diet to be *Artemisia sieversiana* (a member of the sagebrush/wormwood/mugwort family).[3] Gerbils forage widely and hoard seeds in burrows for times of resource scarcity.

Gerbils average 40-80 grams at adulthood and have a body length of 118-138 milimeters, with a haired tail adding another 95-115 milimeters in total length. Gerbils have been described as diurnal, nocturnal and crepuscular but are most likely to have a bimodal activity pattern, with the activity periods linked to specific events such as dawn or dusk in the wild.[4,5,6] Gerbils do not hibernate. In the wild, the animals are generally agouti, but a variety of colors are seen in domesticated animals, including non-agouti, pink-eyed, acromelanic albino ("Siamese"), and albino.[7]

In the wild, animals live together as pair-bonded reproductive adults with juveniles and subadults remaining in the group to assist in parental care. They live in a complex burrow system with multiple entrances and exits. Adjacent territories may be held by related family groups, with overlapping burrow systems. Both males and females defend territory. As a desert animal, gerbils have excellent water conservation mechanisms and produce small, dry feces and scant amounts of urine. Scent-marking in the gerbil is accomplished primarily by rubbing area in the territory with the ventral marking gland (*Figures 1 and 2*).

The gland produces a yellow, musky sebaceous product. The ventral gland is larger in males than females, and males show increased marking behavior when compared to females.[8]

Gerbils kept in captivity today have their origins in a subset of 20 wild pairs captured in 1935 by D. C. Kasuga in the basin of the Amur River. Dr. Kasuga sent these wild gerbils to the Kitasato Institute, Shirokane, Tokyo, Japan, where they were

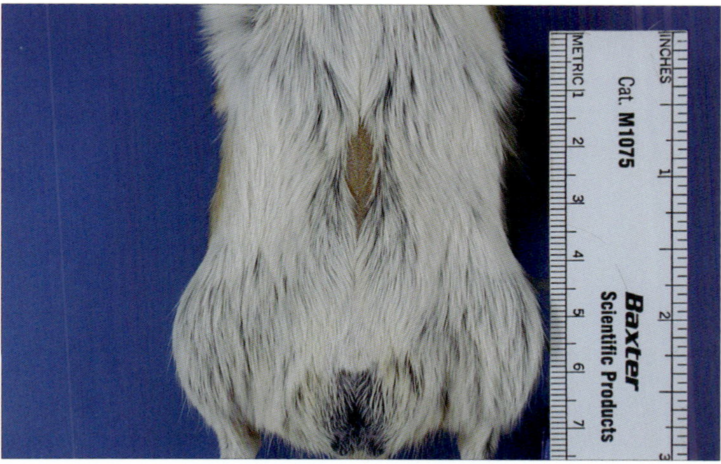

Figure 1: The ventral marking gland in a male gerbil. The gerbil produces scent marks by rubbing this gland on areas within its territory. Both male and female gerbils have ventral marking glands. Charles River, 2012

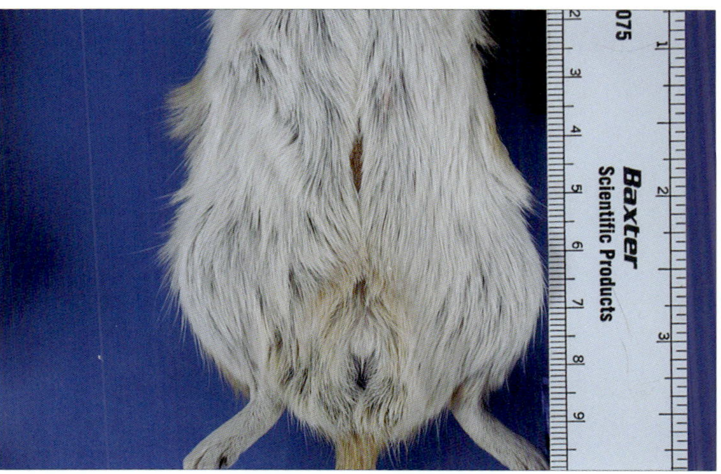

Figure 2: The ventral marking gland in a female gerbil. Compare the size of this gland to the size of the male's.
Charles River, 2012

raised and studied. In 1949, offspring of the original animals were transferred to M. Nomura at the Central Laboratories for Experimental Animals in Japan. Most of the gerbils used in research today descend from a further subset of animals, when either 4 pairs of gerbils and their offspring or 11 pairs of gerbils (accounts differ) were transferred in 1954 to Dr. Victor Schwentker at Tumblebrook Farms in New York. Only 5 females and 4 males of the 11 pairs of gerbils bred, and the closed colony of Tumblebrook Farms was descended from those 9 animals. Tumblebrook Farms was acquired by Charles River in 1995. Gerbils used in research today are considered domesticated rodents as they differ allometrically and genetically from wild gerbils.[9,10]

In current research, gerbils are used as models of ischemic brain injury and epilepsy, and the study of hearing and the development of the structures of the ear. They also play a role in the study of some infectious diseases of humans, such as *Helicobacter pylori*. Relative to mice and rats, very few gerbils are used in research.

Normal Behavioral Repertoire

Eating and drinking

In the wild, gerbils forage for food and then hoard it in their burrows.[3,11] Females hoard more than males, and food deprivation will induce an increase in food hoardng.[12,13] In the laboratory, gerbils are often fed from wire bar cage lids and not given the opportunity to forage for food in the bedding and assemble a hoard. Gerbils fed on the floor of the cage or by J-feeders were significantly heavier when compared to those fed from hanging wire feeders, but reproductive parameters did not differ between groups.[14] Gerbils appear to be adequately nourished on a standard mouse chow diet in the laboratory, but sunflower seeds are valued by the animal if added to the diet.

Grooming

The fixed action pattern of autogrooming in gerbils is similar to that in mice and rats. Self-grooming occurs in a fixed order: mouth/nose, face, ears, flank, ventrum, tail.[15] The grooming pattern in gerbils spreads saliva and Harderian gland secretions on the body. Different types of autogrooming are seen at different temperatures.[15] This may serve as an aid in temperature regulation in the temperature extremes of the gerbil's natural habitat, as saliva serves to cool the gerbil and Harderian gland secretions insulate the pelage against wetness and cold when the temperature drops.[15] Allogrooming is also seen in gerbils, especially between mated pairs, but in the wild rarely occurs outside of burrows.[3,16] Allogrooming is solicited from the groomer by the groomee by a subordinate approach characterized by head lowering with ears back and eyes partially closed. The potential groomee would then freeze and wait for grooming to commence. If this did not work, the groomee may nudge the groomer with the nose and wait or present the part to be groomed.[16] Gerbils will also sandbathe when given the opportunity. In this case, the gerbil will roll repeatedly in a sandy area, burrowing the nose under the sand and rolling from side to side.

Reproductive.

Gerbils form mated pairs, but these are loosely monogamous. Mating in gerbils is related to territory and territory defense. Males establish a territory through marking and chasing of other males. A female will investigate territories, come to prefer a male or a territory, and after developing a preference, a mated female will defend her territory from other females.[17] Females have been observed mating with males from other territories at territorial boundaries, however.[11,17] Based on behavior when the territorial mate is removed, it is postulated that the male gerbil pair-bonds in a way the female does not.[18,19]

As with other rodents, the mating sequence of gerbils follows a pattern.[5,20,21] Males are more likely to approach females and initiate nose-to-nose contact, although many of the solicitation behaviors preparatory to mating are initiated by the estrous female.[21] A male approaching an estrous female may show a particular arousal behavior known as thumping or drumming. This is the rapid patting of the large hind feet on the ground and is seen in other contexts, such as when the animal is startled, but is most commonly associated with reproductive behaviors.

If the female is not receptive, agonistic behavior is likely to follow an approach by a male. If the female is receptive, she is likely to allow anogenital sniffing. The female may also sit on her haunches, presenting her back to the male, and erect the hairs of her lower back. The female then darts away from the male and the male follows. Darting is seen in other rodents as part of copulatory behavior and is described as a short flight away, with a pause, and a subsequent resumption of running. If she is not entirely receptive, there may be further agonistic encounters at this point. Eventually she stops darting away from the male and crouches, immobile and in a lordotic posture. The male is then allowed to mount. She may dart away again during the sexual encounter; this intromission pacing is also important to reproduction in other species of rodents. The male mounts repeatedly, only achieving intromission intermittently. The male may complete as many as 50 intromissions before ejaculation occurs.[20] At the time of ejaculation, the male may drum his feet again, and is likely to clean his genitals immediately after ejaculation.

After a 24- to 26-day gestation period, the female gives birth in a sitting posture, resting on the rump with the hind legs splayed, or in a quadrupedal posture with the hind legs extended.[16] The postpartum estrus occurs 8 to 11 hours after parturition in gerbils.[22] It is fertile, but delayed implantation is probably seen under conditions of resource scarcity or while nursing a litter.[23] Females show increased locomotor activity during estrus, and this is true during the postpartum estrus as well.[22]

Parental

Gerbils gather nesting material, process it, and build nests, especially females close to parturition.[5,24,25] Although male gerbils do not help with parturition, they are active parents and influence the development of offspring.[26,27,28] Both males and females spend a great deal of time in direct bodily contact with pups when housed in captivity, and the association with the ventral marking gland may help to identify pups as belonging to specific parents or even function as a brood patch.[25,29,30] Females sniff and lick pups more often than males, but neither sex shows a high frequency of pup retrieval when pups are not deliberately separated from the nest.[25,31] When males are removed from the cage, females spend more time in contact with pups and build more structurally complex nests, perhaps indicating that the males serve as a crucial heat source for pups.[28] Pup development is well-summarized in Kaplan and Hyland.[32]

In captivity, gerbils are weaned at 28 days, but in the wild, subadults remain in the family burrow until or unless they are expelled by the parents. The subadults do perform "aunting" behaviors such as licking, sniffing and retrieving pups.[33,34] Since gerbils remain in family groups, the reproductive maturation of the subadult males and females is retarded by the presence of familiar adult males and females.[33,35,36] Remaining in the natal group also significantly suppresses infanticide in female gerbils, but not in males, which rarely exhibit that behavior.[33] Eventually, most female and male offspring are expelled from the family group, usually by the dominant female.[37]

Territorial and Agonistic Behaviors

As noted earlier, familial groups of gerbils maintain and defend a territory comprised of an area above ground and a burrow system. Gerbils mark their territory through the use of their ventral marking glands, as well as with sebaceous glands found on their chins and via deposition of feces and urine. The ventral marking gland is unique to the gerbil and has been a frequent object of study by scientists. Scent marking appears to be an innate behavior in gerbils, as gerbils reared by mice and isolated from other gerbils after weaning still scent mark.[38] The behavior begins between 50 and 78 days of age in male gerbils.[38,39] When an animal is marking, it exhibits a particular posture, with the ventrum pressed to the ground and the four limbs extended. The tail is often slightly elevated as are the tarsal surfaces. The animal then drags its belly briefly along the ground or the dorsum of another animal. The dominant male scent marks on rocks, mounds of earth, and other protuberances in a naturalistic environment, and on the bedding substrate or floor in captivity. Males investigate scent marks left by other males more frequently than those of females.[40] Dominant males mark more frequently than subordinate males[3,40] and sexually active males mark more frequently than virgin males.[41]

Agonistic behavior in gerbils is similar to that in other rodents.[16,42] Aggressive interactions can be seen as 1) mediated, in which there is aggression from one animal followed by submission, appeasement, or escape from another animal, or 2) escalated, in which aggressive postures are returned with aggressive postures and fighting ensues, or in which the subordinate animal cannot remove itself from the sight of the aggressor. In general, dominating or aggressive behaviors involve elevating postures, erect ears, staring, direct approaches and chasing. Subordinate or submissive postures involve lowering the body, flattening the ears, closing the eyes, averting the head, freezing and fleeing. Two strange male gerbils meeting for the first time display a sequence of possible behaviors beginning with investigation (anogenital sniffing), then progressing to agonistic postures such as head-up, ears-forward quadrupedal threat postures, displays of the side of the body, rearing on the hind legs and boxing with the forefeet.[16,43] Some of these postures may also be seen as defensive behaviors; for example, if one gerbil rears and begins boxing the other, the second gerbil may defend itself in a similar manner. Agonistic postures can progress to agonistic acts, given the right animals and circumstances. In gerbils, some agonistic acts seen in the wild and in captivity are rushing at another animal, biting a fleeing animal, sparring (in which both gerbils box with the forefeet), displays in which gerbils sidle toward each other and, finally, a locked fight in which both gerbils are biting and scratching.[16,43]

Observing/Quantifying Behavior

Observations of gerbils can be performed via focal sampling (concentration on one individual for a varying length of time, typically measured in minutes), or scan sampling (observation of a larger number of animals for a short period, typically measured in seconds). In focal sampling, the entire behavioral repertoire of one animal may be followed, but sampling multiple animals requires a significant time investment. In scan sampling, data on larger numbers of animals is obtained, but unless animals are individually identified, it is impossible to follow sequences or sets of behaviors.

Gerbils, like many other rodents, move quickly. Because
of this, observation is often facilitated by filming them, then
observing the film in slow motion. Juvenile animals often move
more slowly, so direct observation of preweanling animals and
mothers can often be accomplished in the home cage. Affiliative
and agonistic behaviors are often quick sequences, so filming
these behaviors may allow for their "unpacking" into discrete
behavioral units.

After deciding how to sample the behavior of the animals
observed, the next question is which behaviors to record. Is it
necessary to record all behaviors or is a focus on only certain
types of behaviors more appropriate? Most importantly, how will
these behaviors be defined? With gerbils, many scientists have
studied their behavior, and clear, repeatable definitions of many
common behaviors can be found in their literature. Many of
these useful references will be discussed below.

One of the best tools in conducting and recording observations
is the ethogram. As mentioned in previous chapters, an
ethogram is a list of behaviors performed by an animal. An
ethogram is most useful when it has an organizing structure,
rather than just an arbitrary list of behaviors. Ethograms are
commonly organized as checklists or flowcharts. In checklists,
behaviors are defined and then grouped in sets by relatedness.
For example, there might be a list associated with sexual
activity, a separate list associated with feeding and a third
list associated with parental behavior. The number of lists is
limited only by the number of behaviors and ways they can be
grouped. A flowchart indicates which behaviors lead to other
behaviors and gives the observer a sense of sequence and
relatedness, rather than a simple list (*Figure 3*).

For example, an ethogram of gerbil development can be found
in Kaplan and Hyland (1972).[32] There is a list of 14 potential
behaviors for mothers and 21 potential behaviors for pups.
Although the behaviors are not linked together in a flowchart,
they are described temporally, with the frequency of behaviors
increasing (locomotion) or decreasing (nursing) over time
as the pups matured. Another ethogram used by Elwood in
1975 focused on 10 behaviors in adult animals rearing pups.[25]

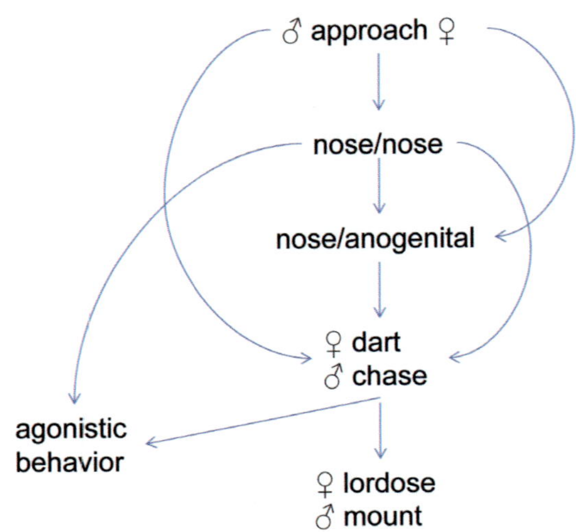

Figure 3: An example of a flow-chart ethogram. This particular ethogram links events in the gerbil copulatory sequence. The arrows indicate the possible behavioral sequences observed by the investigators. In this case, arrows do not return up the sequence, although that is possible with some sequences of behaviors. Size of connecting lines or size of behavioral boxes may indicate relative frequencies of behaviors. Redrawn from Roper and Polioudakis, 1977.[5]

The most complete gerbil ethogram found by this author was contained in a master's thesis by Margaret Moore Platt, entitled "An ethogram of the Mongolian gerbil, *Meriones unguiculatus*."[16] In this work, the author observed animals maintained in a laboratory colony from 1965-1972. Animals were individually identified and followed for up to three years. Behavior was recorded on paper and on tape, and supplemented with video and still photography. Behaviors were classified in general terms as individual or maintenance behaviors or as social behaviors. Another excellent description of behaviors seen in gerbilline rodents is found in Eisenberg.[43]

Although there is much literature on behavior unique to gerbils, such as scent marking with the ventral abdominal gland,[44] gerbils will also perform in the standard rodent behavioral testing apparati, such as radial mazes,[45] and testing paradigms, such as intruder/resident testing. Caution should be used, however, if attempting testing involving water, as the desert-dwelling gerbil is not a natural swimmer, showing hesitancy when presented with water and tiring quickly,[16] although Morris water-task testing of gerbils is described in the literature.[46]

Behavioral Management

Enrichment

Social: As gerbils are social animals in the wild,[3,47] living in multi-male/multi-female groups, group housing may be a valuable enrichment. One study of individually housed laboratory gerbils showed an increase in anxiety measured by elevated plus maze in males, but the opposite in the social interaction test. Females showed no anxiety differences in the elevated plus maze, but had increased anxiety, as measured by freezing and less exploration, in the social interaction test.[47] Group-raised laboratory gerbils may benefit from social housing; however, individual experience may influence compatibilities.

Occupational: Occupational enrichments are intended to fulfill a species-specific behavioral need or drive. Generally, these are designed based upon time-budget studies and aim to provide substrate that the animal would normally spend a large portion of their time either searching for, processing or utilizing. Second to social housing for social species, these enrichments tend to be the most valuable to welfare, as they accommodate and encourage species-specific activity and fill idle time in a way that the animal can control.

• Nesting material: Gerbils actively interact with nesting material and will build nests with it, even in single-sex groups or when individually housed.[24] Gerbils will shred and build with straw, paper or wood, and will spend more time chewing thicker paper than thinner,[24] a positive characteristic for enrichments intended to be occupational.

• Sand: Sand is a natural digging substrate for gerbils in the wild[3] and they may[48] or may not[49] prefer it over wood bedding. The ability to dig in sand that did not result in a burrow did not reduce the incidence of stereotypic digging.[48,49] It is possible that soil better suited for burrow building, such as peat or clay, may be beneficial in this regard. However, biosecurity concerns in using such a substance for bedding in the laboratory make this impractical. Gerbils do sandbathe, however; a behavior common to rodents in arid environments[43] and marked by digging followed by rubbing of the ventrum, back and sides in the substrate. Sandbathing has the dual function of dressing the pelage and marking,[43] and so serves both a physiologic and social function. A sand "box" in which to bathe or mark, rather than sand as a digging substrate, may have some value, assuming that sanitation issues could be resolved.

- Foraging opportunities: Gerbils forage extensively in the wild, then hoard the food in group stores.[11] Adults as well as juveniles of both sexes will participate in this behavior, and while generally seasonal in the wild, the behavior can be induced out of season in both wild and domesticated gerbils through the provision of hoardable food. Hiding the food may make the gerbils more motivated to forage.[50] Feeding on the floor of the cage or providing some other foraging mix hidden in the bedding can be a valuable enrichment in captivity.

Physical Enrichment: Physical enrichments generally provide either structural complexity or are meant to encourage increased utilization of the enclosure. Care must be taken when applying these enrichments, making sure to predetermine what behavioral change is desired, and performing observations to confirm that the increased positive utilization of the environment is the result of the physical enrichment, and not increased unwanted or abnormal behaviors.

- Running wheels: Gerbils will utilize running wheels;[6,53] however, the activity appears to be nocturnal (as opposed to normal diurnal behavior patterns)[6] and poorly correlated with food deprivation, suggesting that it is a maladaptive searching strategy for gerbils and may in and of itself be a stereotypy.[51]

- Tubing with a burrow chamber: Gerbils have a strong drive to burrow. However, as previously mentioned, the provision of sand for digging did not alleviate the development of stereotypic digging behaviors.[48,49] Providing a tube with a burrow chamber did, if provided early enough, significantly decrease stereotypical digging, the most common abnormal behavior observed in this species.[49,52,53]

Recommended Environment/Behavioral Husbandry Program

Although domesticated gerbils exhibit a full range of wild behaviors when housed in naturalistic settings, fully or semi-naturalistic desert housing is unrealistic in most cases in the laboratory.[5] Larger cages do not affect the development of stereotypic digging, the primary stereotypy seen in gerbils, so their provision may not be necessary.[54] However, in many areas gerbil cage size is regulated by law, so the addition of any item that takes up cage space may require a larger cage to meet floor size recommendations.

At a minimum, a gerbil's enclosure should have a solid bottom, be bedded with a wood product, allow the gerbil to stand on the hind legs with head fully erect and contain nesting material. Ideally, the cage would also allow the opportunity to forage for food and construct food hoards,[55] have a burrow chamber with an L-shaped entrance,[56] perhaps contain a running wheel and have an area in which the gerbil could sandbathe.

References

1. Milne-Edwards, A. Observations sur quelques mammifères du nord de la Chine. *Annales des Sciences Naturelle* .**V**, 375-377 (1867).

2. Musser, G. & Carleton, M. in *Mammmal Species of the World* (eds. Wilson, D. & Reeder, D.). (The Johns Hopkins University Press, Baltimore, 2005).

3. Ågren, G., Zhou, Q. & Zhong, W. Ecology and social behaviour of Mongolian gerbils, Meriones unguiculatus, at Xilinhot, Inner Mongolia, China. *Animal Behavior.* **37**, 11-27 (1989).

4. Pietrewicz, A. T., Hoff, M. P. & Higgins, S. A. Activity rhythms in the Mongolian gerbil under natural light conditions. *Physiol Behav.* **29**, 377-380 (1982).

5. Roper, T. J. & Polioudakis, E. The behaviour of Mongolian gerbils in a semi-natural environment, with special reference to ventral marking, dominance, and sociability. *Behaviour.* **61**, 207-237 (1977).

6. Weinert, D., Weinandy, R. & Gattermann, R. Photic and non-photic effects on the daily activity pattern of Mongolian gerbils. *Physiol Behav.* **90**, 325-333 (2007).

7. Petrij, F., van Veen, K., Mettler, M. & Brückmann, V. A second acromelanistic allelomorph at the albino locus of the Mongolian gerbil (Meriones unguiculatus). *Journal of Heredity.* **92**, 74-78 (2001).

8. Whitsett, J. M. & Thiessen, D. D. Sex difference in the control of scent-marking behavior in the Mongolian gerbil (Meriones unguiculatus). *J Comp Physiol Psychol.* **78**, 381-385 (1972).

9. Stuermer, I. W. et al. *Intraspecific allometric comparison of laboratory gerbils with Mongolian gerbils trapped in the wild indicates domestication in* Meriones unguiculatus (Milne-Edwards, 1867) (Rodentia: Gerbillinae). Zoologischer Anzeiger. 249-266 (2003).

10. Neumann, K. et al. Low microsatellite variation in laboratory gerbils. *Journal of Heredity.* **92**, 71-74 (2001).

11. Ågren, G., Zhou, Q. & Zhong, W. Territoriality, cooperation and resource priority: hoarding in the Mongolian gerbil, *Meriones unguiculatus. Animal Behavior.* **37**, 28-32 (1989).

12. Nyby, J. & Thiessen, D. D. Food hoarding in the mongolian gerbil (*Meriones unguiculatus*): effects of food deprivation. *Behav Neural Biol.* **30**, 39-48 (1980).

13. Nyby, J., Wallace, P., Owen, K. & Thiessen, D. D. An influence of hormones on hoarding behavior in the Mongolian gerbil (*Meriones unguiculatus*). *Horm Behav.* **4**, 283-288 (1973).

14. Mulder, G. B., Pritchett-Corning, K. R., Gramlich, M. A. & Crocker, A. E. Method of feed presentation affects the growth of Mongolian gerbils (*Meriones unguiculatus*). *J Am Assoc Lab Anim Sci.* **49**, 36-39 (2010).

15. Thiessen, D. D. Body temperature and grooming in the Mongolian gerbil. *Ann N Y Acad Sci.* **525**, 27-39 (1988).

16. Platt, M. M. 754 (Cornell, 1977).

17. Ågren, G. Pair formation in the Mongolian gerbil. *Animal Behaviour.* **32**, 528-535 (1984).

18. Starkey, N. J. & Hendrie, C. A. Importance of gender for the display of social impairment in pairbond disrupted gerbils. *Neurosci Biobehav Rev.* **23**, 273-237 (1998).

19. Starkey, N. J. & Hendrie, C. A. Disruption of pairs produces pair-bond disruption in male but not female Mongolian gerbils. *Physiol Behav.* **65**, 497-503 (1998).

20. Kuehn, R. E. & Zucker, I. Reproductive behavior of the Mongolian gerbil (Meriones unguiculatus). *Journal of Comparative and Physiological Psychology.* **66**, 747-752 (1968).

21. Burley, R. A. Pre-copulatory and copulatory behavior in relation to stages of the estrous cycle in the female Mongolian gerbil. *Behaviour.* **72**, 211-241 (1980).

22. Prates, E. J. & Guerra, R. F. Parental care and sexual interactions in Mongolian gerbils (*Meriones unguiculatus*) during the postpartum estrus. *Behav Processes.* **70**, 104-12 (2005).

23. Marston, J. H. & Chang, M. C. The breeding, management and reproductive physiology of the Mongolian gerbil (Meriones unguiculatus). *Lab Anim Care.* **15**, 34-48 (1965).

24. Glickman, S. E., Fried, L. & Morrison, B. A. Shredding of Nesting Material in Mongolian Gerbil. *Perceptual and Motor Skills.* **24**, 473-474 (1967).

25. Elwood, R. W. Paternal and maternal behavior in the Mongolian gerbil. *Anim Behav.* **23**, 766-772 (1975).

26. Clark, M. M. & Galef, B. G., Jr. Effects of experience on the parental responses of male Mongolian gerbils. *Dev Psychobiol.* **36**, 177-185 (2000).

27. Piovanotti, M. R. A. & Vieira, M. L. Presence of the father and parental experience have differentiated effects on pup development in Mongolian gerbils (*Meriones unguiculatus*). *Behavioural Processes.* **66**, 107-117 (2004).

28. Elwood, R. W. & Broom, D. M. Influence of litter size and parental behavior on development of Mongolian gerbil pups. *Animal Behaviour.* **26**, 438-454 (1978).

29. Ostermeyer, M. C. & Elwood, R. W. Helpers (?) at the nest in the Mongolian gerbil, *Meriones unguiculatus*. *Behaviour.* **91**, 61-77 (1984).

30. Kittrell, E. M., Gregg, B. R. & Thiessen, D. D. Brood patch function for the ventral scent gland of the female Mongolian gerbil, *Meriones unguiculatus*. *Dev Psychobiol.* **15**, 197-202 (1982).

31. Waring, A. & Perper, T. Parental behavior in the Mongolian gerbil (*Meriones unguiculatus*). 1. Retrieval. *Animal Behaviour.* **27**, 1091-1097 (1979).

32. Kaplan, H. & Hyland, S. O. Behavioural development in the Mongolian gerbil (Meriones unguiculatus). *Animal Behaviour.* **20**, 147-154 (1972).

33. Saltzman, W. et al. Effects of siblings on reproductive maturation and infanticidal behavior in cooperatively breeding Mongolian gerbils. *Dev Psychobiol.* **51**, 60-72 (2009).

34. Scheibler, E., Weinandy, R. & Gattermann, R. Social categories in families of Mongolian gerbils. *Physiol Behav*. **81**, 455-464 (2004).

35. Clark, M. M. & Galef, B. G., Jr. Socially induced delayed reproduction in female Mongolian gerbils (*Meriones unguiculatus*): is there anything special about dominant females? *J Comp Psychol*. **116**, 363-368 (2002).

36. Saltzman, W. et al. Social suppression of female reproductive maturation and infanticidal behavior in cooperatively breeding Mongolian gerbils. *Horm Behav*. **49**, 527-537 (2006).

37. Scheibler, E., Weinandy, R. & Gattermann, R. Intra-family aggression modulates physiological features of the Mongolian gerbil *Meriones unguiculatus*. *Acta Zoologica Sinica*. 51, 989-997 (2005).

38. Arkin, A. et al. Marking behavior is innate and not learned in the Mongolian gerbil. *Exp Anim*. **49**, 205-209 (2000).

39. Lindzey, G., Thiessen, D. D. & Tucker, A. Development and hormonal control of territorial marking in the male Mongolian gerbil (*Meriones unguiculatus*). *Dev Psychobiol*. **1**, 97-99 (1968).

40. Thiessen, D. D., Lindzey, G., Blum, S. L. & Wallace, P. Social interactions and scent marking in the Mongolian gerbil (*Meriones unguiculatus*). *Animal Behaviour*. **19**, 505-513 (1971).

41. Shimozuru, M., Kikusui, T., Takeuchi, Y. & Mori, Y. Scent-marking and sexual activity may reflect social hierarchy among group-living male Mongolian gerbils (*Meriones unguiculatus*). *Physiol Behav*. **89**, 644-649 (2006).

42. Ginsburg, H. J. & Braud, W. G. Laboratory investigation of aggressive behavior in Mongolian gerbils (*Meriones unguiculatus*). *Psychonomic Science*. **22**, 54-55 (1971).

43. Eisenberg, J. F. A comparative study in rodent ethology with emphasis on social behavior, I. *Proceedings of the United States National Museum*. **122**, 1-50 (1967).

44. Thiessen, D. & Yahr, P. *The gerbil in behavioral investigations: mechanisms of territoriality and olfactory communication* (University of Texas Press, Austin, 1977).

45. Wilkie, D. M. & Slobin, P. Gerbils in space: performance on the 17-arm radial maze. *Journal of the Experimental Analysis of Behavior.* **40**, 301-312 (1983).

46. Zhang, Y. B. et al. Neuroprotective effects of N-stearoyltyrosine on transient global cerebral ischemia in gerbils. *Brain Res.* **1287**, 146-156 (2009).

47. Starkey, N. J., Normington, G. & Bridges, N. J. The effects of individual housing on 'anxious' behaviour in male and female gerbils. *Physiology & Behavior.* **90**, 545-552 (2007).

48. Pettijohn, T. F. & Barkes, B. M. Surface choice and behavior in adult Mongolian gerbils. *Psychol Rec.* **28**, 299-303 (1978).

49. Wiedenmayer, C. Causation of the ontogenetic development of stereotypic digging in gerbils. *Animal Behaviour.* **53**, 461-470 (1997).

50. Forkman, B. The Foraging Behaviour of Mongolian Gerbils: A Behavioural Need or a Need to Know? *Behaviour.* **133**, 129-143 (1996).

51. Sherwin, C. M. Voluntary wheel running: a review and novel interpretation. *Animal Behaviour.* **56**, 11-27 (1998).

52. Wiedenmayer, C. Stereotypies resulting from a deviation in the ontogenetic development of gerbils. *Behavioural Processes.* **39**, 215-221 (1997).

53. Waiblinger, E. & Koenig, B. Housing and husbandry conditions affect stereotypic behaviour in laboratory gerbils. *Altex-Alternativen Zu Tierexperimenten.* **24**, 67-69 (2007).

54. Wiedenmayer, C. Effect of cage size on the ontogeny of stereotyped behaviour in gerbils. *Applied Animal Behaviour Science.* **47**, 225-233 (1996).

55. Sørensen, D. B. et al. An ethological approach to housing requirements of golden hamsters, Mongolian gerbils and fat sand rats in the laboratory—A review. *Applied Animal Behaviour Science.* **94**, 181-195 (2005).

56. Waiblinger, E. in *Comfortable Quarters for Laboratory Animals* (eds. Reinhardt, V. & Reinhardt, A.). 18-25 (Animal Welfare Institute, Washington, D.C., 2002).

DATE SUBMITTED: _______________________________________

DATES OF STUDY: START: _____________________   END: _____________

PROJECT TITLE: [   ]

SITE/ROOM(S) WHERE CONDUCTED:

Site: ___________________________________   Room: _________________

ANIMAL STRAIN, SPECIES, WEIGHT/AGE, SEX:

Animal Strain	Species	Weight	Age	Sex

The following list of questions should be borne in mind when designing an environmental enrichment device, and revisited again once the device is constructed. The list should be consulted both during initial observations following the introduction of the device, and during ongoing observations of the device as it remains in use. The safety assessment of an enrichment device does not stop once it has been safety tested; safety testing should be seen as a continuous process because of wear and tear on devices, and because animals may discover unexpected ways of using a device.(Note: These questions were adapted from the cited references.)[1,2,3]

1. Does the device have any sharp edges? ☐ Yes ☐ No

2. Can the animal's digits, limbs, or other bodily appendages become trapped inside any part of the device? ☐ Yes ☐ No

3. Is it likely that the animal could break the device? ☐ Yes ☐ No

4. If the device could be broken, would it break into sharp fragments and/or would the constituent parts of the device pose a safety risk? ☐ Yes ☐ No

5. Could the device be dismantled by the animal? ☐ Yes ☐ No

6. If the device could be dismantled, would any constituent parts pose a safety risk? ☐ Yes ☐ No

7. Can the device or any part of it be swallowed? ☐ Yes ☐ No

8. Is the device made of non-toxic material? ☐ Yes ☐ No

9. Could the animal gnaw pieces off the device? ☐ Yes ☐ No

10. Can the device be cleaned adequately or sterilized to prevent disease transmission? ☐ Yes ☐ No

11. Can the animal in any way become entangled in the device? ☐ Yes ☐ No

12. Could the animal use the device as a weapon against cagemates, caregivers or other people? ☐ Yes ☐ No

13. Could the animal use the device to damage its enclosure? ☐ Yes ☐ No

14. Could the animal use the device to facilitate escape from its enclosure? ☐ Yes ☐ No

Besides safety, the following questions can also help determine the feasibility of a new enrichment device:

1. Can the device be filled and maintained quickly? ☐ Yes ☐ No
2. Does the installation of the device block any caregiver access or restrict view of the animals? ☐ Yes ☐ No
3. Does use of the device require the caregiver to enter the enclosure? ☐ Yes ☐ No
4. Is the device of the simplest design possible? ☐ Yes ☐ No

Product testing before distribution to the animals should include:

1. Drop test (one meter onto concrete is standard)
2. Sharp seams & edge test
3. Strength of the attachments (i.e., Can parts be pulled off?)
4. Strength of the seams

PLEASE INDICATE THE RESULTS OF THESE INITIAL TESTS HERE:

NATURE AND POTENTIAL BENEFIT OF THE PROPOSED ENRICHMENT DEVICE:
Please include manufacturer, if the item can be certified, if/where it is in use elsewhere, and a picture of the device where at all possible.

DESCRIPTION OF HOW THE ASSESSMENT OF THE ITEM WILL BE PERFORMED:
What criteria will be documented, what the monitoring program and frequency will be, etc.

ANIMAL NUMBERS & JUSTIFICATIONS FOR NUMBERS AND SPECIES CHOSEN:

RESULTS:

Results will be reported back to ________________ upon completion.

SUMMARY/ OUTCOME:

Adapted from multiple sources.[1,2,3]

References

1. Baer, J. F. "A Veterinary Perspective of Potential Risk Factors in Environmental Enrichment" in *Second Nature: Environmental Enrichment for Captive Animals* (Zoo and Aquarium Biology and Conservation Series) (eds D. J. Shepherdson, J. D. Mellen, & M. Hutchins). 277-301 (Smithsonian Institution Press, 1998).

2. Bielitzki, J. Letter to the Editor: Enrichment Hazards. *Laboratory Primate Newsletter*. **31**, 36 (1992).

3. Young, R. *Environmental Enrichment for Captive Animals*. 62-67 (Blackwell Publishing Company, 2003).

**Notes